Chinese
Wisdom

Chinese Wisdom

Philosophical insights from
Confucius, Mencius, Laozi, Zhuangzi
and other masters

Edward L. Shaughnessy

Photographs by
John Cleare

DUNCAN BAIRD PUBLISHERS
LONDON

Chinese Wisdom
Edward L. Shaughnessy

First published in the United Kingdom
and Ireland in 2010 by
Duncan Baird Publishers Ltd
Sixth Floor, Castle House
75–76 Wells Street
London W1T 3QH

Conceived, created and designed by
Duncan Baird Publishers

Managing Editor: Christopher Westhorp
Managing Designer: Clare Thorpe
Picture Editor: Julia Brown

British Library Cataloguing-in-Publication Data:
A CIP record for this book is available from the
British Library

ISBN: 978-1-84483-915-5

10 9 8 7 6 5 4 3 2 1

Typeset in Present and Skia
Colour reproduction by Colourscan, Singapore
Printed in China by Imago

Notes:
The Pinyin system of romanization has been
used throughout.

The source texts are cited without a definite
article, thus it is *Analects* or *Laozi* rather than
The Analects or *The Laozi*.

Abbreviations used throughout this book:
CE Common Era (the equivalent of AD)
BCE Before the Common Era (the equivalent
 of BC)
c. circa (approximately), r. reigned.

Contents

Preface   6

Introduction   8

The Wisdom   32

    Family   34

    Education   50

    Warfare   72

    The Dao   90

    Government   106

    Sagehood   132

    Death   158

Index   174

Further reading   176

About the author/photographer   176

Preface

As my two young daughters, Giulia and Maria, approach the age of reason, I find myself wishing to explain to them that the books that I spend my days reading are filled not just with strange looking writing, but also with considerable wisdom about what it means to be human. What is more, as I have watched both them and me grow over these last nine years, I have come to realize ever more clearly the truth of one of the fundamental notions of ancient Chinese thought: that while we are all born with the potential to grow into fully evolved human beings, that growth requires time and—more important—requires also encounters with the diverse situations of life, especially life in human society. Cute as they are, there is nothing more self-centered than newborn babies. Then, through playing with others, little by little they learn to share. A little later they take their first steps outside of their own family; most of the most important things that they learn in their first years of school are not in their schoolbooks, but in their relationships with teachers and classmates. This is just the start of a lifetime of discovery and growth. At some point they will probably, like their father, find themselves first in subordinate positions in society, in which they will have certain obligations to their superiors, and then later in positions of responsibility, in which they have very different obligations to their subordinates. If they are lucky enough, they will become parents, and, again like their father, will find that the learning curve does not stop at all with adulthood. Indeed, parents may well learn more from their children than their children do from them, at least about the things that really matter. This is perhaps why Chinese philosophers have always regarded family relationships—all the family relationships, the love the parent has for the child as well as the respect the child should have for the parent and also the various responsibilities that the elder sibling and the younger sibling have vis-à-vis each other—as the basis of society. There may be especially gifted individuals who can understand what life is all about entirely on their own, but most of us learn little by little as we move through the stages of life.

And so I have organized this book of quotations from the philosophical writings of China's classical age according to the stages of life: infancy and notions of the family; adolescence and education; early adulthood and warfare (whether they become soldiers or not, young adults often find themselves thrust into battles of one kind or another); maturity and government (whether as leaders of states or just as heads of departments at work, if we are lucky enough to survive the battles of early adulthood, we are often asked to assume ever greater responsibilities); old age and the wisdom that we hope it brings to us; and finally death, which is certain to come to all of us and about which all of us wonder at various points in our lives. I hope that the quotations in this last section show that this need not be a frightening conclusion to life. In the middle of these reflections on the stages of life, I have placed a section on the *dao* (often written *tao*) or the Chinese "Way." Not all of the writers quoted agree on any of these topics, but it seems to me that all of them have something to tell us. I hope that some day soon my two little girls will read and appreciate these writings. For now, however, dear reader, the book is in your hands.

Introduction

Chinese of all periods and all philosophical persuasions have agreed in calling the way of the world and the way of life the *dao* (better known in the West as *tao*). The word was by no means used only by those thinkers, such as Laozi (traditionally dated to the sixth century BCE) and Zhuangzi (*c.*365–285BCE), who have come to be known as Daoists. It was used just as well, and in much the same sense, by Confucius and his followers. Indeed, even the later thinkers who in the West are conventionally called Neo-Confucians originally referred to their pursuit as "the study of the *dao*."

Like most Chinese characters, the standard character for the word *dao* is usually written with two elements, one sometimes known as the "stop-and-go" element showing a foot on a road, and one portraying the human head. This second element was probably mainly intended to indicate the pronunciation of the word, but many believe it also added meaning to it, perhaps indicating the direction that one was "headed" on the road. A delicious example of this understanding is found, for instance, in the late Professor Peter Boodberg's translation of the famous first line of the *Laozi* or *Dao De Jing* (the *Classic of the Way and Virtue*), usually rendered as something like "The way that can be spoken is not the eternal way." Boodberg, a scholar of the most rigorous standards but also one with a twinkle in his eye, rendered the line "Lodehead lodehead brooking, no forewonted lodehead."

Fun as "lodehead" might be for *dao*, most translators are content to translate the word as "way," sometimes capitalizing it ("Way") when it refers to the Way of the world or the one Way to lead one's life, perhaps unconsciously drawing a parallel to the pronouncement of Jesus that "I am the Way and the Life." In recent years, the "headless" interpretation of *dao* has received unexpected support in the way the word was written in manuscripts from the ancient period. Over the last two decades, archaeologists have discovered numerous manuscripts of all sorts dating from the fourth century BCE. In these, the word *dao* is often written with the familiar combination of the "stop-and-go" element and the head, but a not uncommon variant displays a "man" on a "road." From this it is even clearer that the road is what gives the word its meaning.

Except perhaps in Kansas, roads are not always straight and easy to follow. Typically they twist here to avoid a rock outcropping, or turn there to take advantage of a natural corridor. In line with this, there is good reason to think that that same first line of the *Laozi* was originally understood to mean something like "The way that can lead (or be followed) is not a constant way." This line, which in the original reads literally "*dao* can *dao* not constant *dao*," points to two other important features of the Chinese language. First, most words can be used as either nouns or verbs; thus *dao* can mean both "road" and "to be on the road." Second, at least in the written language, many verbs that involve exchange between two parties originally did not differentiate between the direction in which the exchange took place. Thus, the word *shou* could mean either "to give" or "to receive"; the word *mai* meant either "to buy" or "to sell." Similarly, the word *dao*, used as a verb in the sense of showing direction, could mean either "to lead" or "to follow." In a certain sense, whether the road "leads" or we "follow" it makes no difference. The important thing is to be on the road.

The road as a metaphor for the way of life works especially well in an educational context. Confucius (551–479BCE), the first of all Chinese teachers, exemplified in his sayings and his personal conduct the twists and turns of the Way, often responding in very different ways to the same question posed by different students. Of course, he did not leave behind a handbook explaining his teaching method, but it seems clear that he recognized that each of his students had individual talents and needs, some responding well to encouragement while others required discipline and restraint. It is probably also the case that he intentionally resisted pat answers to difficult questions, preferring instead to revisit them from different perspectives, hoping eventually to give—and to get—a fuller understanding of all the issues involved.

This flexibility that characterizes many classical Chinese teachings ought not to be mistaken for any sort of moral relativity. There are certain core values at the heart of most teachings. For Confucius probably the most important of these is the word *ren* (*jen*), variously translated by others as "benevolence," "goodness," "man-to-manness," "man-at-his-best," and so forth, but which I render below as either "humaneness" or "humane," depending on the part of speech. With this translation I seek to preserve the connection in Chinese between this word and another word also pronounced *ren*, and usually translated as "man" or "person," but which simply indicates "human" (as a noun, for example, "human beings" as opposed to animals or ghosts and spirits). By "humane" I intend what it means to be fully human.

As in the case of the word for *dao* or "Way," so too in the case of *ren* have the manuscript discoveries of the last two decades provided new insights into its meaning. In conventional Chinese script, the virtue *ren* is written with a combination of the graph for the word *ren* meaning "human" and the graph for "two." It is often explained that "humaneness" derives from and is manifest in the interactions between two or more people, such that one can only be "humane" by engaging in the human community. For this reason, the hermit hiding himself away from society and thereby preserving his purity was not a desirable model for most classical Chinese thinkers. This is in part because of the need to share one's abilities with others, almost a moral imperative to influence others for the better (Confucius and many others regarded such influence as a necessary result of the humane person's interactions with others).

Confucius's most celebrated statement on what it means to be *ren* or "humane" came in response to a question from his favorite disciple Yan Hui (521– 481BCE). Confucius said:

> To overcome the self and return to the rites is to be humane. If for one day one overcame the self and returned to the rites, all under heaven would return to humaneness from this. To be humane comes from the self, but oh, think of what comes from humaneness!

ANALECTS

The "rites" (*li*) is another term often encountered in classical Chinese texts, one perhaps off-putting to many modern Western readers who understand it to be the

rituals of another time and place. I think this is a serious misunderstanding. For Confucius, the rites were all of the ways in which human interaction takes place. True enough, it included for him the monthly sacrifice of a sheep, something that in his own day brought the family members together but which has little relevance for us today. But his conception of the rites might well be extended to include knowing when to greet an acquaintance with a firm handshake or with a kiss on the cheek. In all cases, the basis of correct performance of the rites lies in "overcoming the self," in getting beyond selfishness and self-consciousness to be able to identify with the other.

Indeed, in another place Confucius proposed that the ability to identify with the other was the single most important thing that he had to teach.

> Zi Gong asked, "Is there a single saying that we can put into action throughout our lives?" Confucius said, "Perhaps putting oneself in the other's place. What you don't wish for yourself, don't do to others."

ANALECTS

The single word that I translate here as "to put oneself in the other's place" is *shu*, sometimes translated as "reciprocity," "commiseration" or "sympathy." As in the case of the other words examined above, *shu* too is interesting for the way it is written. It has as its basic component the graph *ru*, which means in its own right "to be like, to resemble," but which derives from a probably earlier word that is the simple pronoun "you." This is placed over a "heart," giving a coherent sense of the emotional identification with another or, as I put it above, "putting oneself in the other's place." Confucius's follow-up makes this clearer still: "What you don't wish for yourself, don't do to others."

The active other-centered focus of these statements by Confucius would certainly be accepted by many other early Chinese philosophers, from the radically egalitarian Mozi (c.478–392BCE) down to Han Feizi (c.280–233BCE), the pragmatic advisor to the ruler who would become the First Emperor of China. However, there is another aspect to being humane as well, an aspect perhaps most fully explored by Confucius's most important disciple, Zengzi (c.505–436BCE). This too begins with the need to help others, but recognizes as well that one's own growth is inextricably tied to that of the others—a more elaborate version of the old saying that when we give to others we get even more in return for ourselves. In the famous formulation of the *Great Learning* (*Da Xue*) attributed to him, bringing peace to the world requires the cultivation of one's own internal dispositions —and vice versa. The way to humaneness is very much a two-way road.

> In ancient times, those who wished to illuminate lustrous virtue under heaven first brought order to their states. Those who wished to bring order to their states first regulated their families. Those who wished to regulate their families first cultivated their persons. Those who wished to cultivate their persons first made their hearts upright. Those who wished to make their hearts upright first made their ideas sincere. Those who wished to make their ideas sincere first extended their knowledge.

Extending knowledge resides in going out to things. Only after you go out to things can your knowledge arrive. Only after your knowledge arrives can your ideas be sincere. Only after your ideas are sincere can your heart be upright. Only after your heart is upright can your person be cultivated. Only after your person is cultivated can your family be regulated. Only after your family is regulated can the state be in order. Only after the state is in order can all under heaven be at peace.

GREAT LEARNING

Manuscripts from China's Warring States period (c.453–221BCE) found in the last two decades provide some support for the turn inward of the word *ren*, at least in the way in which the graph is written. As opposed to the traditional form combining "human" with "two," in the manuscripts the graph is almost always written with either a human being (*ren*) or a human body (*shen*) over a "heart" component. The contexts of these occurrences show that the word expresses the same engagement in the human community, but the "heart" component perhaps brings into the open the emotional or psychological aspect of this engagement.

Another core word in the classical Chinese philosophical vocabulary for which the newly discovered manuscripts provide a new perspective is *yi*. This word has traditionally been translated as "righteousness," "justice" or sometimes "duty" or "responsibility," depending on context, though now it is perhaps more often rendered as "propriety" or "proper," as it is in this book. The new translation is intended to do two things: first to avoid confusion with Judeo-Christian notions of a divine "righteousness," which do not correspond well to the senses of the word in the context of ancient China; and second to draw explicit connections with the basic component of the graph used to write the word in Chinese—*wo* meaning "we." In the conventional Chinese script, *yi* is written with a "sheep," seemingly indicative of most things good or beautiful, over the top of *wo*. This perhaps points toward the good that derives from belonging to a "we-group," what is proper to us. In the manuscripts as well, the word is often written in this form, and so it seems appropriate to maintain the translations "propriety" and "proper." However, the word also appears in another guise, still with the basic component *wo*, but like *ren* now combined with a "heart." This calls to mind an interesting debate in ancient China over whether *yi* belonged to an external standard or to an internal disposition. This ostensibly pitted Gaozi (c.420–350BCE) against Mencius (Mengzi, c.385–305BCE), though since the debate is featured in the book the *Mencius* it is obvious which of the two gets the final word.

> Gaozi said, "Impulses for food and sex are part of our nature. Humaneness is internal while propriety is external; it is not something internal."

> Mencius said, "Why do you say that humaneness is internal while propriety is external?"

> Gaozi said, "That guy is an elder and so I treat him as an elder; it is not just that he is older than I am. This is the same as if he were white and so I regarded him as white, based on his whiteness being on the outside. This is why I say it is external."

Mencius said, "Even if the whiteness of a white horse is no different from the whiteness of a white man, would you not recognize that the elderliness of an elderly horse is different from the elderliness of an elderly man? What's more, which one is acting properly: the one who is elder or the one who treats him as an elder?"

Gaozi said, "If it is the case of my younger brother then I love him, but if it is the case of a younger brother of someone from Qin then I don't love him. In this way it is I who feel the joy, and so I would call it internal. But in the case of treating an elder of Chu as an elder, I would still treat him as my elder, and in this way it is the elder who feels the joy and so I would call it external."

Mencius said, "I like the roast meat of the man of Qin just the same as I like my own roast meat. So things are also like this, but would you then say that my liking roast meat is also external?"

MENCIUS

There were numerous other debates among the ancient Chinese philosophers, not all of them quite so serious as this one between Gaozi and Mencius. The following humorous exchange between Hui Shi (*c.*370–310BCE) and Zhuangzi also played on different senses of a single word, in this case the question word *an*, which can mean either "how" or "where" depending on context.

Zhuangzi and Hui Shi were hiking along the
bridge over the River Hao. Zhuangzi said, "The
minnows darting out there are swimming so
carefree; this is the joy of a fish." Hui Shi said,
"You're not a fish; where do you get off knowing
the joy of a fish?" Zhuangzi said, "You're not I;
where do you get off knowing that I don't know
the joy of a fish?" Hui Shi said, "I am not you, so
surely I don't know you; but you are surely not a
fish, so you totally don't know the joy of a fish."
Zhuangzi said, "Let's go back to the basic premise.
You said to me 'Where do you get off knowing
the joy of a fish,' which shows that you already
knew that I knew it or you wouldn't have asked.
I know it from up here on the River Hao."

ZHUANGZI

The intellectual climate of the Warring States period
was remarkably free, with thinkers experimenting with
different ways to approach the world. I certainly hope
that the discussion above of certain core beliefs common
to most thinkers will not give the impression that all of
them thought the same way or that there is some sort
of unchanging wisdom of the Orient. Nevertheless, it
is certainly the case that some sayings have had greater
influence over later Chinese thinkers than others, and
that some have more universal applicability than others.
It is these eternal sayings that I have tried to capture in
the seven chapters that make up this book.

The writers in this anthology

Before concluding this brief Introduction, it is useful to have a brief survey of the fifteen or so most important of the ancient Chinese thinkers, the ones whose sayings are featured in this book.

Lao Dan or Laozi (traditionally dated to the sixth century BCE)

According to some traditions, Laozi was an elder contemporary of Confucius, and so features at the very beginning of the Chinese philosophical tradition. He is supposed to have left a book called either simply *Laozi* or, perhaps more commonly in the West, the *Dao De Jing* or the *Classic of the Way and Virtue*. As the second title implies, this book is concerned in the first place with the *dao* or the Way and then also with its application in the world, its "virtue." As such, it has long been regarded as the fountainhead of Daoist thought. Throughout the twentieth century, there was a vigorous debate over the historicity of Laozi the man and the date of *Laozi* the book, with perhaps most scholars in the West arguing that he never existed and that the book probably did not reach anything approaching its present form until the third century BCE. In 1993, at a village called Guodian in the central province of Hubei, three different manuscripts dating to about 300BCE were found composed entirely of sayings found in the *Laozi*. Some view these manuscripts as excerpts from a longer text and thus as proof that the *Laozi* is as old as tradition holds, while others see them as a text still in its formative stage. This may well be an example of the classic glass half full or half empty problem. But of two things there can be no doubt: the text is ancient, and it contains wisdom that still speaks to us today.

Kong Qiu or Kongzi or Confucius (551–479BCE)

Confucius is surely the best-known Chinese person of all
time, in China traditionally regarded as the sage for ten
thousand generations. After a brief period of criticism
after the founding of the People's Republic of China, he
has now been restored to his place of honor, with many
localities refurbishing their temples dedicated to him and
the state even establishing Confucius Institutes around the
world. Confucius was born in the eastern Chinese state of
Lu, in what is now Shandong province, and passed much
of his life there. He served a couple of brief stints in the
government of the state, but he never rose higher than the
equivalent of the chief of police. Eventually he dedicated
himself to teaching a group of disciples, some of whom
went on to important government careers and others of
whom became important teachers in their own right. Some
of these disciples, or their own disciples, edited a collection
of Confucius's sayings called the *Lunyu* or *Analects*. In
addition to these quotations of the masters, many other of
his sayings—or at least sayings attributed to him—made
their way into a wide range of other books over the next
several centuries. His thought is known for its equal concern
for both the spiritual and pragmatic sides of life of both
oneself and others, and for the warmth and force of his own
personality, which makes itself felt still today.

Sun Wu or Sunzi (late sixth to early fifth century BCE)

Sunzi (Sun Tzu in Wade-Giles romanization) was a general
from the northeastern state of Qi who, according to his later
biography, first made a name for himself when he trained
the harem of King Helu of Wu (r.514 – 496BCE) to march
in formation. According to this biography, Sunzi formed

the women into two formations, each headed by one of
the king's two favorite concubines. After having instructed
the women in the ways of marching, Sunzi ordered them
to march. When they fell out giggling, he ordered the two
leading concubines to be executed on the spot, horrifying
King Helu. Arguing that a general had absolute command in
the field, he is supposed to have carried out the executions.
Thereafter, the remaining women in the harem obeyed his
every instruction without the least twitter. The book that
goes by his name, *Sunzi*, often with the added title *Art of
War* (*Bing Fa*), is composed of maxims that stress the need
for an army's unity of purpose and stealth in the execution
of warfare. It inspired the guerilla warfare techniques
employed by Mao Zedong in China and by Ho Chi-minh
in Vietnam, and is now frequently quoted even in the
boardrooms of international corporations.

Zeng Shen or Zengzi (c.505–436BCE)

Zengzi was probably the last of the disciples to join
Confucius's circle, being only in his mid-twenties at the time
of the master's death. He eventually came to be recognized
as the leader of at least one faction of Confucians, and seems
to have had a major hand in putting together the *Analects*
of Confucius and thus in forming the picture that we have
of Confucius himself. Credited with the authorship of the
Great Learning (*Da Xue*), which was elevated to the status
of one of the Four Books of Confucianism during the later
Song dynasty (960–1279CE), Zengzi stressed the importance
of internal dispositions over actual performance of rituals.
With the recent discovery of manuscripts at Guodian and
other sites, many Chinese scholars have begun to argue for
his central role in the development of Confucian thought.

Kong Ji or Zi Si (c.483–402BCE)

As the grandson of Confucius, a student of Zengzi, and at least nominally the teacher of Mencius, Zi Si occupies one of the most important places in the development of Confucian thought. Like his teacher Zengzi, he too argued that the heart (and thus also the mind) is the ruler of the body, and that if the heart is pure pure actions naturally follow from it. Also like his teacher Zengzi, Zi Si has been central to the recent reevaluation of the development of the Confucian tradition. Four texts that he is supposed to have written, including the famous *Doctrine of the Mean* (*Zhong Yong*), which like the *Great Learning* was later made one of the Four Books, have been preserved in the *Record of Ritual* (*Li Ji*). More recently, two different manuscript copies of one of these texts, the *Black Jacket* (*Zi Yi*), have been discovered, showing beyond doubt that his teaching was indeed extremely influential by no later than the fourth century BCE.

Mo Di or Mozi (c.478–392BCE)

Although the teaching contained in the book that Mozi is said to have written, the *Mozi*, strikes many modern readers as quite prosaic, within the century in which he died Mencius would write that half of the people in the world were his followers. A fierce opponent of waste in all its forms, Mozi marshaled utilitarian arguments for the greatest good. He is now most famous for his teachings in favor of "universal love" (perhaps better rendered as "impartial love") and against offensive warfare. Not just a philosopher, he organized his disciples into armies, which he took to support states under attack and pioneered defensive weapons that would continue to be used for more than a millennium by cities under siege. These disciples eventually divided into three separate factions, each with its own leader and each with its own version of Mozi's teaching; these organized factions may have been precursors of later widespread millenarian religious movements.

Yang Zhu (c.395–335BCE)

According to the *Mencius*, written in about 320 to 310BCE, the half of the people in the world who did not follow Mozi were followers of Yang Zhu. Other than his characterization by Mencius as an extreme egotist, one who would not pull out even a single hair from his arm in order to benefit the whole world, little is known of his thought. Nevertheless, there are interpretations of this one saying that are both more generous to Yang Zhu and also more interesting philosophically; there is reason to think that one of these interpretations—that in trying to help the world we end up losing our natural bond with it—was very influential in Daoist thought, particularly that of Zhuangzi.

Gongsun Yang or Shang Yang (c.390–338BCE)

A nobleman of the central state of Wey, Shang Yang arrived in the western state of Qin in 361BCE, becoming an advisor to the ruling Duke Xiao (r.381–338BCE). He advised the ruler to establish an authoritarian form of government that took agriculture and military strength as its two supports and quickly transformed Qin from the backward state that it had been into the most militarily powerful state of the age. He also advised Duke Xiao to restrict the privileges of the aristocracy, and to establish in its place a system of ranks based on merit. Finally, he also argued for a code of laws to be established and followed rigorously. Unfortunately for him, with the death of Duke Xiao in 338BCE, the aristocrats of the state exacted their revenge on Shang Yang and had him executed. A book attributed to him and known as the *Shang Jun Shu* or *Book of the Lord Shang* is regarded as the founding document of a political philosophy usually called Legalism.

Shen Buhai (C.400–337BCE)

Shen Buhai was a contemporary of Shang Yang. Like Shang Yang he rose to the rank of chancellor, though Shen served in the central Chinese state of Han. He too is credited with establishing techniques of government, stressing in particular the need for an administrative bureaucracy in which all parts played their particular roles, and in which the ruler would not need to intervene. Although he was subsequently regarded as a Legalist, and his thought did have a certain influence on the later writings of Han Feizi, it would seem that his philosophy might better be described as belonging to the peculiar admixture of Daoism and Legalism called Huang-Lao. The book attributed to Shen Buhai, the *Shenzi*, has long been lost, though there are several editions of quotations of it. Herrlee Creel, one of the great twentieth-century scholars of ancient Chinese thought, attempted to resuscitate Shen Buhai's reputation, arguing that as the father (or at least grandfather) of bureaucracy in China, Shen Buhai was perhaps the most important of all of China's political philosophers.

Meng Ke or Mengzi or Mencius (C.385–305BCE)

Mencius has traditionally been regarded as the second sage of Confucianism, ranking only after Confucius himself in order of importance. Like Confucius, he was born in a small state in eastern China in what is now Shandong province, and like Confucius he tried, generally unsuccessfully, to gain positions as an advisor to the rulers of the various states of his day. His greatest success—in the court of King Xuan of Qi (r.319–301BCE)—proved also to be his greatest failure when a military intervention which Mencius had advocated turned into a disastrous defeat. A follower of the brand of Confucianism espoused by Zengzi and Zi Si, Mencius famously argued that humans are by nature good, and that it is only through contact with the outside world that they come to be corrupted. As such, all people have sagehood within them, and also have the potential to become sages if they but decide to do so. In the Song dynasty, the book of Mencius, the *Mencius*, was made one of the Four Books of Confucianism, and is often regarded as a model for learning the classical Chinese language. It is one of the ancient Chinese books most frequently translated into Western languages.

Zhuang Zhou or Zhuangzi (c.365–285BCE)

The *Zhuangzi*, the book written at least in some part by Zhuangzi, is just about everybody's favorite book from ancient China. Combining a profound insight into the *dao* and its interaction with people with an extraordinary wit and inventiveness in the use of the Chinese language, the parables of the *Zhuangzi* consistently show the folly of what is usually regarded by the world as sense and success. Often paired with the *Laozi* or *Dao De Jing* as the two great classics of Daoism, the *Zhuangzi* teaches the essential interconnectedness of all things. And since all things form part of the one unified *dao*, it is self-defeating to claim ownership of anything for oneself or to try to remain fixed in one point in time. The *Zhuangzi* has been rendered into

English by several of the best translators of classical Chinese, the eloquence of its language setting a challenge to them.

Xun Qing or Xunzi (c.315–220BCE)

Xunzi is usually regarded as the third of the great classical Confucian philosophers. Indeed, through the Tang dynasty (618–907CE), he was probably more highly regarded than Mencius, with whom he is often contrasted because of his famous dictum that mankind is inherently evil. Striking though this dictum is, the goal of Xunzi's teaching is not noticeably different from that of Mencius—the perfectability of humankind. Xunzi stressed that although man starts with selfish desires, he can overcome them through education in the rites that had been established by the sages. Xunzi was probably the greatest essayist of ancient China, and the individual chapters of his book, the *Xunzi*, are the closest thing to analytical philosophy that one will find from that time and place. Most chapters begin with a problem, explore the pros and cons of the issues in detail, and eventually arrive at a conclusion that is almost invariably reasonable, at least within the context of his argument. He probably had more actual influence on the workings of government than any other Confucian philosopher of the period, though ironically this came through two of his students, Han Fei (Han Feizi) and Li Si, both of whom became advisors to the autocratic First Emperor of Qin.

Lü Buwei (290–235BCE)

As a merchant from the state of Wey, Lü Buwei became one of the richest men of his age. He attained the position of chancellor in the state of Qin, serving both King

Zhuangxiang (r.250–247BCE) and then also King Zheng (r.246–221–210BCE), the latter of whom was to become the First Emperor after conquering all of the other states of the day. It is said that he brought together around him three thousand retainers, and he set them the task of writing a book that would encompass all of the knowledge of the world. So pleased was he with the result when they completed the book in 239BCE that he displayed it in the marketplace of the Qin capital, Xianyang, offering ten thousand pieces of gold to anyone who could add or subtract a single word from its excellence. Whether the book is quite so perfect as that, we can certainly say that it is the first of the great Chinese encyclopedias and does serve as something of a summation of all the knowledge of the world then available. Unfortunately for Lü Buwei, shortly after the completion of the book he fell from grace with King Zheng and committed suicide. Fortunately, however, his book, which had long been the only great pre-Han Chinese classic not to be translated into English, is now finally available in an excellent complete translation.

Han Fei or Han Feizi (c.280–233BCE)

Han Feizi was from the ruling family of the state of Han, in central China. At a young age, he studied with the great Confucian philosopher Xunzi. Tradition holds that because he spoke with a severe stutter, limiting his ability to present his viewpoints verbally at the courts of the time, he developed his talent as a writer. And it is certainly true that he became a consummate writer, probably the most elegant stylist in the ancient period. Never influential in his home state of Han, his works eventually came to the attention of King Zheng of Qin, the eventual First Emperor, who arranged for him to be sent to his court as an ambassador. The writings, compiled into a hefty volume called the *Han Feizi*, provide the theoretical underpinning of the political philosophy usually called Legalism. This philosophy is often denounced as countenancing dictatorship, but a sympathetic reading of Han Feizi would place him well within the pragmatic Confucian orbit of his teacher Xunzi. While it is true that he argued for the paramount position of the ruler, this is always presented as the best way to promote the well-being of the people as a whole. Han Feizi's life was to end in tragedy: within a year of his arrival at the Qin court, Li Si (*c.*280–208BCE), a former fellow student of his under Xunzi, slandered him. Unable to defend himself, Han Feizi committed suicide.

The seven chapters that follow collect sayings and stories that these and a few other ancient Chinese writers presented regarding the major topics of family, education, warfare, the *dao*, government, sagehood, and death. Needless to say, these seven topics do not exhaust the wisdom that ancient Chinese texts have for us today, but they do seem to me to be reflective of some of the most important concerns of both that day and of our own day. I am responsible for the selection and arrangement of the quotations, and also for all of the translations, which have all been done anew for this volume.

The Wisdom

Family

The Way of the gentleman is like traveling to a distant place; you must start from what is near. Or like climbing to a high place; you must start from below.

DOCTRINE OF THE MEAN

When it is at rest it is easy to hold onto, and when it has not yet appeared it is easy to plan for. When it is cut up, it is easy to destroy, and when it is tiny it is easy to disperse. Act on it when it has not yet come into being; control it when it is not yet in disorder. A tree two girths round grows from a tiny seed. A terrace nine storeys high begins from mounds of dirt. A journey of a thousand miles starts beneath one's feet.

LAOZI

Although one's parents be dead, if you are about to do something good, think about the fine reputation you will leave for your parents and you will certainly do it; if you are about to do something that is not good, think about the shame you will leave to your parents and you will certainly not do it.

RECORD OF RITUAL

Mencius said, "The Way resides near at hand, and yet people seek it in the distance. The matter is easy, and yet seeking it is difficult. If everyone would treat their parents as parents and treat their elders as elders, then all under heaven would be at peace."

MENCIUS

The Way of the gentleman begins with the husband and wife; as for where it gets to, it is to be found throughout heaven and earth.

DOCTRINE OF THE MEAN

Meng Wubo asked about filial piety. Confucius said, "Let the father and mother's only worry be about your being ill."

ANALECTS

Zi Gong asked, "Is there a single saying that we can put into action throughout our lives?" Confucius said, "Perhaps putting oneself in the other's place. What you don't wish for yourself, don't do to others."

ANALECTS

Confucius was seated, Zengzi waiting upon him. The Master said, "The past kings had a most important way of the utmost virtue to make all under heaven compliant, the people were harmonious and between superiors and inferiors there was no resentment; do you know about it?" Zengzi got up and said, "I am not very bright; how would I know about it?" The Master said, "Filial piety is the root of virtue, that from which education comes to life. Sit back down and I'll explain it to you. Our body, hair, and skin is what we get from our parents; not daring to harm it is the beginning of filial piety. Establishing oneself and moving along the Way, elevating your name for later generations so as to make your parents illustrious is the end of filial piety. Filial piety begins in serving your parents, goes in the middle to serving your lord, and ends with establishing your person. The *Greater Encomia* says: 'Without remembering your ancestors, How would you cultivate your virtue.'"

CLASSIC OF FILIAL PIETY

If the gentleperson is generous with his family, then the people will rise up in humaneness. If old relations are not abandoned, then the people will not be rude.

ANALECTS

The Way of the great learning resides in illuminating lustrous virtue, in drawing near to the people, in stopping in the highest good. Only after knowing to stop can one have stability; only after having stability can one be tranquil; only after being tranquil can one be at peace; only after being at peace can one deliberate; only after deliberating can one succeed.

Things have their roots and branches, affairs have their ends and beginnings. If you know what to put first and last, then you are close to the Way. In ancient times, those who wished to illuminate lustrous virtue under heaven first brought order to their states. Those who wished to bring order to their states first regulated their families. Those who wished to regulate their households first cultivated their persons. Those who wished to cultivate their persons first made their hearts upright. Those who wished to make their hearts upright first made their ideas sincere. Those who wished to make their ideas sincere first extended their knowledge.

Extending knowledge resides in going out to things. Only after you go out to things can your knowledge arrive. Only after your knowledge arrives can your ideas be sincere. Only after your ideas are sincere can your heart be upright. Only after your heart is upright can your person be cultivated. Only after your person is cultivated can your family be regulated. Only after your family is regulated can the state be in order. Only after the state is in order can all under heaven be at peace.

GREAT LEARNING

In the state of Chu there was Honest Gong. His father stole a sheep and he reported him to the authorities. The magistrate said, "Kill him," regarding him as honest to his ruler but crooked with his father, and so the man was punished. Looked at in this way, a ruler's honest minister is a father's vile son. In the state of Lu there was a man who followed his ruler into battle, in three battles running away three times. When Confucius asked him the reason for this, he said, "I have an aged father; if I die there will be no one to take care of him. Confucius regarded him as filial and praised and promoted him. Looked at in this way, a father's filial son is a ruler's disobedient subject.

HAN FEIZI

Youzi said, "There are few indeed who are filial and fraternal in their personal conduct and who enjoy offending their superiors. And there has never been one who did not enjoy offending superiors but enjoyed causing trouble. The gentleman attends to the basics. When the basics have been put in place, then the Way lives. Is it not the case that filial piety and fraternity are the basis of being humane!"

ANALECTS

What is called "ruling the kingdom" must begin with setting the family in order. There has never been a case where one was not able to teach his family and yet was able to teach others. Therefore, the gentleman does not leave his family to teach throughout the kingdom. Filial piety is what is used to serve one's ruler; fraternity is what is used to serve one's elders; parental love is what is used to serve the masses.

GREAT LEARNING

Zengzi said, "When a gentleperson walks down the road, it can be known who his father was and who his teacher was. Without a father and without a teacher, who would I be!" This is to say that serving a teacher is just the same as serving a father.

LÜ SHI CHUNQIU

Cut off the ruler on account of the father, but do not cut off the father on account of the ruler.

GUODIAN MANUSCRIPT "SIX VIRTUES"

Among babes in arms, none does not know to love its
parents. When they grow up, none does not know to respect
its elder brother. Humanity is treating one's parents as
parents. Propriety is respecting one's elders. There is nothing
else but to extend these to the world.

MENCIUS

One who loves his parents would not dare to disdain those
of others. One who respects his parents would not dare to
treat badly those of others. Love and respect find complete
fulfillment in serving one's parents, but virtuous teaching
extends to all people.

CLASSIC OF FILIAL PIETY

If you treat your own aged as the aged ought to be treated
and then extend that to the aged of others, and treat your
own young as the young ought to be treated and then
extend it to the young of others, all under heaven can be
rolled in the palm of your hand.

MENCIUS

Filial piety is what gives birth to education.

CLASSIC OF FILIAL PIETY

All people possess within them a heart that cannot bear the suffering of others. The former kings had a heart that could not bear the suffering of others and so they had a government that would not bear to let people suffer. If one used a heart that cannot bear the suffering of others to put into effect a government that will not bear to let people suffer, then ruling all the world would be as simple as rolling it in the palm of the hand. The reason I say that all people have a heart that cannot bear the suffering of others is that if today people happened to see a small child about to fall into a well, they would all have hearts frightened and saddened. They would be this way not because they wanted to get something from the child's parents, or because they wanted to be praised by the community and their friends, nor because they disliked the sound of the baby crying.

MENCIUS

There was a wealthy man in the state of Song. It rained and the wall of his house was destroyed. His son said, "If you don't fix it, there will certainly be robbers." His neighbor's father said the same thing. That night he really did lose a great part of his wealth. His family regarded his son as extremely intelligent and suspected the neighbor's father.

HAN FEIZI

The way parents are with children and the way children are with parents is like a single body divided into two parts or different breaths of the same air. It is like plants having flowers and fruit or trees having roots and leaves; although they are in different places, they are in communication with each other. If one has hidden desires they will reach the other, if one is ill the other will take care of him, if one is sad the other will feel for her, if one is healthy the other will be happy for him, and if one dies the other will mourn for her. This is what it means to be flesh-and-blood relatives. The spirit comes out of loyalty and responds in the heart and the two essences get each other; what need would there be to say anything!

LÜ SHI CHUNQIU

It is rare to find one who loves and yet still knows another's flaws, or hates and yet still knows another's good points. Therefore, the proverb has it, "No one knows his children's flaws; no one knows how big their seedlings have grown." This means that if one's person has not been cultivated, it is not possible to regulate his family.

GREAT LEARNING

Confucius said to Master Sanghu, "I have twice been expelled from Lu, had trees chopped down on me in Song, had my tracks wiped away in Wei, came to the end of my resources in Shang and Zhou, and was surrounded on the border of Chen and Cai. Why is it that while I have encountered these many troubles my family and relatives have grown ever more distant and my disciples and friends ever more scattered?" Master Sanghu said, "Are you the only one who has not heard of the man who left Jia? Lin Hui cast away a jade disc worth a thousand dollars, put his baby on his back and hurried off. Someone said, 'Did you do it because of the price? But the price of a baby is so small! Or did you do it because of the trouble? But the trouble of a baby is so much! Why would you throw away a thousand-dollar jade piece and hurry off with a baby on your back?' Lin Hui said, 'I was brought together with that one by profit, but I was joined with this one by heaven. Things brought together by profit, when pressed by misfortune and danger, will cast each other aside; but things joined by heaven, when pressed by misfortune and danger, will shelter each other. The difference between sheltering each other and casting each other aside is really distant indeed!'"

ZHUANGZI

Chunyu Kun said, "Is it the ritual that men and women do not touch one another when they give and take things?" Mencius said, "That is the ritual." Chunyu Kun said, "If your sister-in-law were drowning, should you reach out to her with your hand?" Mencius said, "If a sister-in-law were drowning and one did not reach out to her, this would be to be a wild beast. That men and women do not touch one another when they give and take is the ritual; reaching out with the hand to a drowning sister-in-law is weighing things in the balance." Chunyu Kun said, "Today, all under heaven is drowning. Why is it that you, sir, do not reach out?" Mencius said, "When all under heaven is drowning, you reach out to it with the Way. When a sister-in-law is drowning, you reach out to her with your hand. Do you want me to reach out to all under heaven with my hand?"

MENCIUS

Zi You asked about filial piety. Confucius said, "The filial of today talk about being able to provide for their parents. Even dogs and horses are able to be provided for. If not for respect, what would there be to differentiate them?"

ANALECTS

Education

The *Changes* says, "Tying the sack; there is no trouble, there is no praise." Confucius said, "This speaks of shutting the petty person's mouth. When the petty person talks a lot he makes a lot of mistakes, and when he has many activities he has many anxieties. And yet you cannot shut him up through words. It is just like 'tying a pouch'; nothing comes out but nothing goes in."

MAWANGDUI MANUSCRIPT
"THE SEVERAL DISCIPLES ASKED"

Confucius said, "In a town of ten households there will certainly be someone as loyal and trustworthy as I am, but there will be no one who loves to study the way I do."

ANALECTS

When a person is born there are two things that do not need to be learned. The first is to breathe and the second is to eat. Other than these two things, there is nothing that is not the result of learning and habit.

MAWANGDUI MANUSCRIPT
"DISCUSSION OF THE HIGHEST WAY UNDER HEAVEN"

A warped piece of wood must be subjected to straightening and steaming before it will become straight; blunt metal must be subjected to sharpening before it will become sharp. Now, man's nature is evil and must be subjected to a teacher before it will become upright.

XUNZI

Confucius said, "Si, do you take me for one that studies a lot and knows it all?" He replied, "Yes, is it not the case?" Confucius said, "It is not. I link all my studies with one notion."

ANALECTS

Confucius said, "I once spent a whole day without eating and a whole night without sleeping in order to think. There was no gain; it was not as good as studying."

ANALECTS

Confucius said, "Is it not a pleasure to study and in a timely manner put into practice what you have learned? Is it not a joy when friends come from distant places? Is it not a gentleperson who is not bothered if others do not know about him?"

ANALECTS

Zi Gong asked Confucius, "For what will later generations praise my master?" Confucius said, "What would be worth praising about me? If need be, then it would be that I loved to study and was not pressed down by it, loved to teach and was not tired by it; just this."

ANALECTS

That the sons of the hundred craftsmen are capable even without studying is not that they were born clever, but that they have heard about this constantly.

SHEN DAO

If you wish to have a place for yourself you have to give a place to others; if you wish to succeed yourself, you have to help others to succeed.

ANALECTS

Confucius said, "When the gentleperson eats without trying to stuff himself, is at home without seeking rest, is diligent in his work and careful in speech, and stays with those who have the Way and corrects himself against them, this can be said to be the loving of learning."

ANALECTS

Within the four seas, their inner-nature is one. The way they use their hearts is each different, education causing it to be so.

GUODIAN MANUSCRIPT

"THE INNER NATURE COMES FROM THE MANDATE"

Without accumulating little steps, there is no way to reach a thousand miles; without accumulating little streams, there is no way to make a river or a sea. The finest thoroughbred in a single bound is not capable of ten paces, but an old workhorse can be driven for ten days. The result lies in not quitting.

XUNZI

Nature gave birth to people and made their ears able to hear, but without study their hearing is not as good as being deaf; made their eyes able to see, but without study their seeing is not as good as being blind; made their mouths able to speak, but without study their speaking is not as good as being mute; made their minds able to know, but without study their knowing is not as good as being ignorant. Thus, when one studies, it is not that one can increase one's talents, it is that one reaches one's heavenly nature. Being able to keep whole what heaven gives birth to and not to spoil it is what is called being good at studying.

LÜ SHI CHUNQIU

One who knows he is a fool is not the biggest fool; one who knows he is confused is not the most confused. The one who is most confused to the end of his life never gets straightened out; the biggest fool to the end of his life never figures it out. If three men are traveling along and one of them is confused, they can still get to where they are going, because the one who is confused is in the minority. If two of them are confused, then they will work at it and not arrive, because the ones who are confused win out. Nowadays with the world so confused, even though I pray for an echo, I can't get anywhere. Isn't it sad!

ZHUANGZI

There is nothing in the world that does not have both strengths and weaknesses. People are also like this. Therefore, one who is good at learning makes use of the strengths of others to compensate for his own weaknesses. Therefore, one who makes use of others will subsequently come to possess the world.

LÜ SHI CHUNQIU

One who knows does not speak; one who speaks does not know.

LAOZI

I once thought all day, but it wasn't as good as a moment's studying. I once stood on my tip-toes and gazed into the distance, but I didn't see as far as climbing a high place. When one climbs a high place and waves, it's not that your arm has gotten any longer and yet people will see you from afar; when you call out with the wind at your back, it's not that your voice has gotten louder and yet people will hear you clearly. When you make use of a horse and cart, it doesn't make your feet better and yet you can reach a thousand miles; when you make use of a boat and oars, it's not that you can swim and yet you get across rivers and streams. The gentleperson is not different by birth; he is good at making use of things.

XUNZI

The learning of the gentleman enters into his ears, inscribes itself on his heart, spreads through his four limbs, and takes shape in his actions. Every utterance or movement can serve as a model. The learning of the petty person enters his ears and comes out of his mouth. Since the distance between the mouth and the ears is no more than four inches, how could it suffice to embellish a seven-foot tall body. In ancient times people studied for themselves; today people study for others.

XUNZI

One who criticizes me and is right is my teacher; one who
agrees with me and is right is my friend; but one who
flatters me is my thief.

XUNZI

Confucius said, "Animating the old and knowing the new,
one can be a teacher."

ANALECTS

Zi Gong asked, "How did Kong Wenzi get the title '*wen*'
[cultured]?" Confucius said, "He was diligent and loved to
study, and was not ashamed to ask his inferiors questions.
This is why he was called *wen*."

ANALECTS

If three people travel then they will lose one person. If one
person travels then she will gain her friend.

YI JING

Is not to know it to know? Is to know it not to know? Who
knows the knowing that does not know?

ZHUANGZI

Confucius said, "The gentleperson seeks within himself, the petty person seeks from others."

ANALECTS

To make a mistake and not to correct it, this is really what is called a mistake.

ANALECTS

Confucius said, "When I see the worthy I hope to emulate them, and when I see the unworthy I inspect myself within."

ANALECTS

Confucius said, "From those who bring a bundle of dried meat on up, I have never not taught anyone."

ANALECTS

Sages are born from quickness to study; there has never been a case of one who was not quick to study being able to make a name for himself. Quickness to study resides in honoring a teacher; if one honors a teacher, your words will be trustworthy and your way in order.

LÜ SHI CHUNQIU

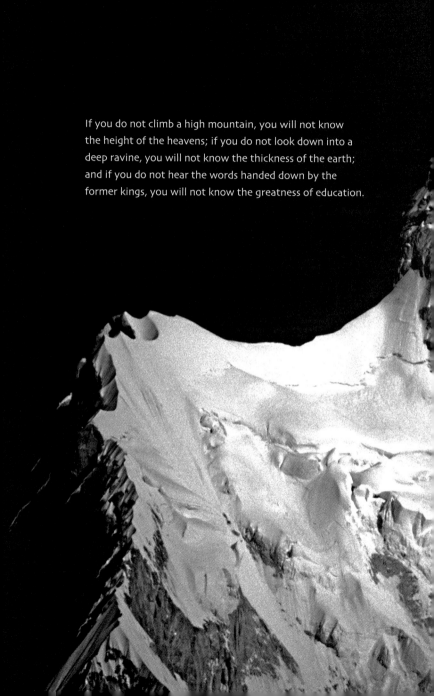

If you do not climb a high mountain, you will not know the height of the heavens; if you do not look down into a deep ravine, you will not know the thickness of the earth; and if you do not hear the words handed down by the former kings, you will not know the greatness of education.

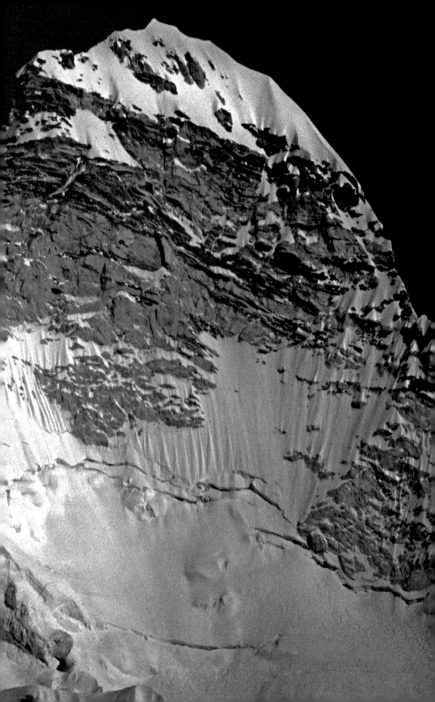

Once when Mencius was young, having quit studying he returned home. His mother, who was just in the midst of sewing, asked him: "Where did you get to in your studying?" Mencius said, "Where I felt like it." His mother took a knife and cut her thread. Mencius was afraid and asked her why. His mother said: "Your quitting your studies is like my cutting this thread. A gentleman studies to establish a name; when asked he knows widely. This is why when he is at home he is at peace and when he travels he stays far from harm. Now if you quit it, you won't avoid being a common laborer and won't stay out of trouble. How is it any different from a woman making a living by sewing, if in the middle of it she quits and doesn't do any more, and yet still wishes to be able to clothe her husband and never be at a lack for food? Such a woman throws away what feeds her, but a man lets slip the cultivation of his virtue; if he does not become a poor bandit, then he will be a prison laborer." Mencius was afraid, and morning and night was diligent in his studies without cease. He took Zi Si as his teacher, and subsequently became one of the world's most famous scholars.

LIE NÜ ZHUAN

A carpenter or a wheelwright can give another his compass or t-square, but he cannot make another skillful.

MENCIUS

Duke Huan was reading a book up in his court. Wheelwright Pian was chiseling a wheel down in the courtyard. He put down his mallet and chisel and went up and asked Duke Huan, "Might I ask what words are those that you are reading?" The duke said, "The words of the sages." He said, "Are the sages in it?" The duke said, "They are already dead, of course." "In that case, then what milord is reading is nothing more than the dregs of the men of old!" Duke Huan said, "Where does a wheelwright get off criticizing the books that I read? If you have an explanation, then OK; if not, then you die!" Wheelwright Pian said, "As for your servant, I look at it from the point of view of my own work. Chiseling a wheel, if I go too slow then it is sweet but not sturdy; if I go too fast, then it is bitter and won't go in. Not too slow and not too fast, I get it in the hand and feel it in the heart; my mouth can't put it in words, but there is an art to it somewhere. I can't illustrate it to my son, and he can't receive it from me. This is why I've gone along for seventy years and have always chiseled wheels. The men of old died together with what they couldn't hand down. This being so, what milord is reading is nothing but the dregs of the men of old."

ZHUANGZI

One who wishes to judge others must first judge himself.

LÜ SHI CHUNQIU

Gaptooth asked Wang Ni, "Do you know what makes things the same?" He said, "How would I know that?" "Do you know what you don't know?" "How would I know that?" "Then, do things have no knowledge?" "How would I know that? Nevertheless, let me try to put it into words. How do I know that what I call 'knowing' is not 'not knowing,' or what I call 'not knowing' is not 'knowing'? What's more, let me try to ask you, if a person sleeps in the damp then his midriff hurts and he is half paralyzed, but is this so of a loach? If he perches in a tree then he is scared out of his wits, but is this so of a monkey? Of these three, which knows the right place to live? People eat meat, deer eat grass, crickets like snake eggs, and raptors munch mice. Of these four which knows the right taste? Monkeys mate with monkeys, deer with deer, and fish sport with fish. Mao Qiang and Li Ji are regarded by men as beautiful, but fish would dive into the depths, birds would fly way up, and deer would run off at the sight of them. Of these four which knows the right beauty in the world? From my point of view, the beginnings of humaneness and propriety and the paths of right and wrong are all balled up together; how would I know how to untangle them!"

ZHUANGZI

Chen Kang asked Confucius's son Bo Yu, "Have you heard anything different from the rest of us?" Bo Yu responded, "Not much. Once [my father] was standing alone, and as I hurried through the courtyard, he said, 'Have you studied the *Poetry*?' I responded, 'Not yet,' to which he said, 'If you don't study the *Poetry*, you will have nothing with which to speak.' I withdrew and studied the *Poetry*. On another day he was again standing alone, and as I hurried through the courtyard, he asked, 'Have you studied the *Rites*?' I responded, 'Not yet,' to which he said, 'If you don't study the *Rites*, you'll have no place to take a stand.' I withdrew and studied the *Rites*. I have heard these two things." Chen Kang withdrew and happily said, "I asked about one thing and learned three; I heard about the *Poetry*, I heard about the *Rites*, and I also heard about a gentleman's putting his son at a distance."

ANALECTS

Study cannot come to an end. Blue is gotten from the indigo plant but is bluer than the indigo plant. Ice is made of water but is colder than water. Wood as straight as a plumb line can be bent into a wheel, its diameter as true as a compass. Even if it is dried, it will not straighten out again. The bending has made it that way.

XUNZI

Missing even one in a hundred shots is not enough to be called good at archery; falling short of a thousand-mile course by even half a step is not enough to be called good at driving. Not linking up relations and categories and not uniting humaneness and propriety is not enough to be called good at learning. Learning is just learning to unite them all. Going out this way and in that way is what the man of the streets does, being good at a few things and not good at many things; this is the likes of Jie, Zhou and Robber Zhi. Only by completing it and seeing it through to the end is it learning.

XUNZI

Learning begins with being a person of breeding and ends with being a sage. If you really accumulate effort for a long time, you will arrive. Learning stops only upon reaching death. Therefore, learning has many ends but one cannot quit for an instant. To do it is to be human, to quit it is to be a beast.

XUNZI

Confucius said: "Knowing it is not as good as loving it; loving it is not as good as delighting in it."

ANALECTS

The reason why one person's wisdom surpasses another's
is because of their having a long view or a short view.
The present is to the past just as the past is to future
generations. And the present is to future generations
just as the present is to the past. Therefore, if you examine
and know the present, you can know the past, and if you
know the past you can know the future. The present and
the past, what comes before and what comes after are all
the same. Therefore, the sage knows back one thousand
years and knows forward one thousand years.

LÜ SHI CHUNQIU

The use of the fish trap lies in the fish; when you have
gotten the fish, forget the trap. The use of the rabbit snare
lies in the rabbit; when you have gotten the rabbit, forget
the snare. The use of words lies in meaning; when you
have gotten the meaning, forget the words. Where can
I get someone who has forgotten words and have a word
with him?

ZHUANGZI

Knowledge is knowing when you know it, and when you
don't know it.

ANALECTS

When the gentleman has reached the stage of loving learning, his eyes will love it more than the five colors, his ears will love it more than the five sounds, his mouth will love it more than the five flavors, and his heart will regard it as more valuable than all under heaven. This is why power and profit cannot sway him, the masses cannot move him, and the whole world cannot sweep him off his feet. He lives and dies for this one thing, which is called virtuous comportment. Only after having reached virtuous comportment can he be settled, and only after being settled can he respond. Able to be settled and able to respond, he is called a complete man.

XUNZI

A man once said, "How great Confucius is! He has studied widely and yet there is nothing for which he has made a name for himself." Confucius heard this, and said to his disciples, "What shall I take up? Shall I take up charioteering? Or shall I take up archery? I will take up charioteering!"

ANALECTS

Not forgetting past events makes one the master of future events.

RECORDS OF THE GRAND HISTORIAN

The root of the orchid is made into perfume, but if it were soaked in urine then the gentleperson would not go near it and the commoner would not wear it. It is not that the thing itself is not beautiful; it is the soaking that has made it so. Therefore, at home the gentleperson necessarily selects where he lives, and in traveling necessarily goes together with men of breeding, so as to resist the evil and mean and draw near to the fair and upright.

XUNZI

Confucius said, "Let there be education without discrimination."

ANALECTS

It is not knowing it that is hard; it is making use of what you know that is hard.

HAN FEIZI

Confucius said, "When three people travel, there is sure to be my teacher among them. I choose that which they do well and follow it, and that which they do not do well and change it.

ANALECTS

Humanity is the heart of man, and propriety is the road of man. What a pity it is when one quits his road and does not follow it, and lets his heart get away and does not know to look for it. When people have chickens and dogs that get away they know to look for them, but they do not know to look for a heart that has gotten away. The way of education is none other than this: it is looking for one's heart that has gotten away.

MENCIUS

Confucius said, "I am not one who knew it from birth. I am one who loves antiquity and strives to seek it."

ANALECTS

To study and not to think is a waste, but to think and not to study is dangerous.

ANALECTS

Warfare

One should view others' kingdoms as he views his own kingdom, view others' households as he views his own household, and view others' persons as he views his own person. Thus, if the lords loved each other they would not fight in the wilds, if the heads of households loved each other they would not extort from each other, and if individuals loved each other they would not mug each other. If lords and ministers loved each other, then they would be generous and loyal, if fathers and sons loved each other they would be caring and filial, and if elder and younger brothers loved each other they would be concordant and harmonious. If the people in the world all loved each other, then the strong would not grab the weak, the many would not oppress the few, the rich would not ridicule the poor, the honored would not be arrogant with the humble, and the crafty would not cheat the dimwitted. All the different problems and oppressions and resentments and hatreds in the world could be made not to arise just by loving each other. This is why the humane praise it.

MOZI

As for a sage's governance of the state, he unifies rewards, unifies punishments, and unifies education. Unifying rewards then the army will have no enemies. Unifying punishments then commands will go into effect. Unifying education then the inferiors will obey the superiors.

SHANG JUN SHU

The basis of using troops and attacking others lies in uniting the people.

XUNZI

The deliberations of the wise necessarily consider both the benefit and the harm. Considering the benefit one's responsibility will be trustworthy, and considering the harm one's anxieties will be resolved.

SUNZI

One who both knows the other and knows himself will never be in peril in a hundred battles. One who does not know the other but knows himself will win some and lose some. One who knows neither the other nor himself will certainly be defeated every time he fights.

SUNZI

A just campaign is one in which a superior attacks an inferior. Enemies do not wage just campaigns against each other.

MENCIUS

Of old those who were good at being soldiers were not warlike, those who were good at fighting were not angry, those good at defeating the enemy did not contend, those good at using humaneness took the lower position. This is called the virtue of not contending; the strength of using others, and being a match for the epitome of heaven.

LAOZI

As for the art of using troops, I do not rely on the enemy's not coming; I rely on being ready for them. I do not rely on their not attacking; I rely on having no place that can be attacked.

SUNZI

Know your adversary and know yourself, and then the victory will not be in peril. Know the heavens and know the earth, and then the victory can be complete.

SUNZI

A hundred victories in a hundred battles is not the best of the best. To bend the other's troops without a fight is the best of the best.

SUNZI

King Xiaocheng and the lord of Linwu asked about generalship. Xunzi said, "In knowledge there is nothing more important than discarding doubt, in action there is nothing more important than having no mistakes, and in serving there is nothing more important than having no regrets. If you get to the point that in your service there are no regrets, then success isn't necessary."

XUNZI

Deliberations must precede affairs and be extended with reverence. Be as careful of the end as of the beginning, and the beginning and end will be as one. This is what is called great auspiciousness. The success of all affairs necessarily lies in having reverence for them.

XUNZI

The epitome of forming troops is to arrive at being formless.

SUNZI

The place where I will join battle cannot be made known. If it is not known, then the places the enemy will have to defend will be many, and if the places the enemy has to defend are many then there will be few of them to join battle with us.

SUNZI

Battle is the art of deceit. Thus, when you are able, show them that you are unable; when you are in motion, show them that you are not in motion; when you are near, show them that you are far; when you are far, show them that you are near. When the enemy is sharp, entice him; when he is disordered, take him; when he is solid, defend against him; when he is strong, avoid him; when he is angry, provoke him; when he is humble, flatter him; when he is rested, belabor him; and when he is intimate with you, put him at a distance. Attack where he has no defenses; come out where he does not expect you.

SUNZI

Victorious troops are first victorious and only afterwards seek a fight; defeated troops fight first and only afterwards seek victory.

SUNZI

A battle formation resembles water. Just as water's form is to avoid the high and rush to the low, so too does the form of troops avoid the solid and hit the empty. Just as water regulates its flow according to the land, so too do troops regulate their tactics according to the enemy. Therefore, the army that has no fixed manner just as water has no fixed formation, but can transform itself according to the enemy and take the victory, is called divine.

SUNZI

One who advances without seeking fame and withdraws without avoiding shame, who only wishes to protect the people and benefit the ruler is a national treasure. If he looks on the troops like they were his babies, they will charge deep ravines with him; if he looks on the troops like they were his loving sons, they will go to the death with him. But if he is generous and unable to employ them, loving and unable to command them, disordered and unable to put them in order, they will be like spoiled brats and he won't be able to use them.

SUNZI

In warfare I have heard of clumsy haste, but I have never seen cleverness drawn out, and there has never been a case of a state benefiting from drawn-out warfare.

SUNZI

The Chu army had not yet completely crossed the river. The Field Marshal said: "Their army is larger than ours; I beg leave to hit them before they have finished crossing." The duke said: "That is not acceptable." When they had already crossed but were not yet drawn up in battle formation, the Field Marshal asked again, but the duke said: "It is still not acceptable." Only after they had drawn up in battle formation did he attack them, and the Song army was defeated in a rout, with the duke wounded in the thigh and the ducal guard all killed. The people of the kingdom all blamed the duke, but the duke said: "The gentleman does not wound twice, does not capture the grey-haired, and the generals of old did not take advantage of defiles. Although I am the survivor of a lost kingdom, I would not sound the attack against an unprepared enemy." Zi Yu said: "Milord does not know anything about warfare. When a mighty enemy is in a ravine and not prepared, this is heaven's present to us; of course it is acceptable to block them and sound the attack; what would there be to be worried about! What's more the mighty armies of today are all our enemies. Even if it were a matter of the aged, we should grab and take them prisoner, much less the grey haired. If you understand shame and seek to teach about warfare, you seek to kill the enemy. If you have wounded them and they haven't yet died, why would you not do it a second time; if you begrudge wounding them twice, then you ought not wound them the first time."

ZUO ZHUAN

As for a country that uses force, if we use our strength to defeat the cities and armies of others, then many of their people will certainly be wounded, and if many of their people are wounded then the hatred of their people for us will certainly be great, and if their hatred for us is great then day by day they will want to fight with us. If we use our strength to defeat the cities and armies of others, then many of our own people will certainly be wounded, and if many of our own people are wounded then the hatred of our own people for us will certainly be great, and if the hatred of our own people for us is great, then day by day they will want to fight with us. If both other people and our own people want daily to fight with us, this is how the strong end up being weak. Lands may come but the people will depart; troubles will pile up and yet the results will be few. Even though what he has to guard increases, what he has to guard it with decreases; this is how the great are chiseled away. All of the other states will remember the relations and meet them with resentment, and will not forget their enemy. They will look for the great country's cracks and take advantage of its being worn out; this is the time of peril for the great and strong.

XUNZI

Annexation is easily accomplished; it is only the consolidating of it that is difficult.

XUNZI

Mencius appeared in audience before King Xiang of Liang. Coming out, he said to another, "When I looked at him from afar he did not resemble a ruler of men, and when I approached him I did not see anything of awe in him. He asked me abruptly, 'How can all under heaven be settled?' I replied saying, 'It is settled through unity.' 'Who can unite it?' I replied saying, 'One who takes no pleasure in killing people can unite them.' 'Who can give it to him?' I replied saying, 'No one under heaven would not give it to him. Does Your Majesty know about rice plants? If in the summer

there is a drought, the seedlings will be parched. But if
clouds rise thick in the heavens and the rain pours down,
then the seedlings will suddenly rise up. Like this, who could
control it? Nowadays, there are no rulers under heaven who
do not take pleasure in killing people. If there were such a
one, the people under heaven would all stretch their necks
to look at him. If he were truly like this, the people would
come to him just as water flows downwards—pouring down,
who could control them?'"

MENCIUS

The states of Han and Wei were fighting and invading each other's land. Master Huazi had an audience with Lord Zhaoxi of Han, who had a worried look on his face. Master Huazi said, "If now the world were to write an inscription in front of you that said, 'If you grab it with your left hand you will lose your right hand; if you grab it with your right hand you will lose your left hand, and yet the one who grabs it will certainly have all under heaven,' would you be able to grab it?" Lord Zhaoxi said, "I would not grab it." Master Huazi said, "Very good! Looked at in this way, your two arms are more important than all under heaven, and your body is even more important than your two arms. The state of Han is also less important than all under heaven and what you are fighting about now is far less important than Han, yet you obstinately trouble yourself and endanger your life because you can't get it!"

ZHUANGZI

Don't advance against a high cliff; don't meet an enemy with its back to a hill; don't follow an enemy that fakes a retreat; don't attack crack troops; don't eat enemy bait; don't block troops that are going home; in surrounding troops necessarily leave an opening; and don't press an enemy that's at its end. This is the art of using troops.

SUNZI

In going to battle, victory is valued, but if the battle
drags on, then the weapons will be blunted, if you attack
citadels then your strength will be bent, and if you expose
your troops for long then the country's resources will be
insufficient. When your weapons are blunted, when your
strength is bent and your resources used up, then the rulers
of other states will take advantage of your being worn out
and will rise up. Even the wisest would not be able to make
anything good out of the aftermath.

SUNZI

A country is impoverished by its army when there are
distant supply lines; if there are distant supply lines then
the common people will be impoverished.

SUNZI

In general, the art of using troops is first to keep one's
own country whole; smashing the enemy comes second.

SUNZI

In general, in battle, one meets the enemy head-on but
wins with the unusual.

SUNZI

In general, in raising an army of 100,000 men and going out on a campaign of 1,000 miles, the cost to the common people and the public purse will be a thousand pieces of gold a day. At home and abroad there will be demonstrations and unrest in the streets, and 700,000 households will not be able to attend to their business. One will be engaged for several years in order to win a single day's victory and yet will begrudge medals and rewards that cost just a hundred pieces of gold. Not knowing the condition of the enemy is the height of inhumanity; this is not the general of the people, not the assistant to the ruler, and not the master of victory. Therefore, the reason why the enlightened ruler and the wise general can defeat others when they move and achieve success from the masses is because of advance knowledge. Advance knowledge cannot be gotten from the gods, cannot be pictured in events, and cannot be modeled in calculations; it has to be gotten from people, those who know the condition of the enemy.

SUNZI

Zi Lu said, "If you were to put the Three Armies in motion, who would you have with you?" The Master said, "I would not have anyone who fights tigers or fords rivers, who could die and not regret it. If necessary, it would be someone who looks on events with dread and who is good at planning and finishing things."

ANALECTS

When Lord Wu of Wei was occupying the state of Zhongshan, he asked Li Ke, "Why is it that the state of Wu came to an end?" Li Ke responded, "Many battles and many victories." Lord Wu said, "Many battles and many victories is the good fortune of a state. Why is it that it alone came to an end?" He responded, "If there are many battles then the people become fatigued, and if there are many victories then the ruler becomes arrogant. It's rare indeed to have an arrogant ruler using fatigued people and the state not being lost."

LÜ SHI CHUNQIU

Weapons are instruments of ill omen, not the instruments of the gentleman. If he cannot avoid using them, lightly is best. Thus, he does not regard them as something of beauty. If he were to regard them as something of beauty, this would be to take joy in killing others. One who takes joy in killing can never get his way in the world. ... When a battle has been victorious, one treats it with a mourning ceremony.

LAOZI

One who uses the Way to be the ruler of others does not use weapons to force the world, because these things tend to return. Where troops are located, brambles grow. Therefore, one who is good at it achieves the result and stops, and does not take a position of strength.

LAOZI

Now there is a man who enters another's orchard and steals his peaches and pears. If the masses heard about this they would condemn him, and if the government caught him it would punish him. Why is this? Because he harms others to benefit himself. Coming to snatching another's dogs and pigs, chickens and piglets, his impropriety is even greater than entering another's orchard and stealing his peaches and pears. Why is this? Because his harm of another is even more, so his inhumaneness is still greater and his guilt is increased. Coming to entering another's stable and taking his horses and cows, his inhumaneness is greater still than snatching another's dogs and pigs, chickens and piglets. Why is this? Because his harm of others is even more. Coming to killing an innocent man, stripping his coat and clothes, taking his battle-ax and sword, his impropriety is greater still than entering another's stable and taking his horses and cows. Why is this? Because his harm of another is even more. If he has harmed the other even more, then his inhumanity is still greater and his guilt is increased. Now, the rulers under heaven all know this and condemn it, and call it improper. But coming to something as great as attacking another kingdom, then they do not know to condemn it, but instead praise it and call it proper. Can this not be said to be the difference between knowing what is proper and improper?

MOZI

The Dao

The Way has reality and truth but is without action or
form. It can be handed on but not received, can be obtained
but not seen. It is its own root and its own stem. Before
there was heaven and earth, from of old it firmly existed.
It inspirited the ghosts and ancestors, gave birth to heaven
and earth. It was before the Great Ultimate and yet is not
high; it is below the six directions and yet is not deep; it was
born before heaven and earth, and yet is not long-lived; it is
longer than high antiquity and yet is not old.

ZHUANGZI

The highest excellence is like water. Water excels at
benefiting the ten thousand things and does not contend
with them; it occupies the places that the masses of men
disdain. Therefore, it is near to the Way.

LAOZI

You pray for rain and it rains; why is this? I say it is for no
reason at all; it is just the same as if you hadn't prayed for
rain and it rained.

XUNZI

One who holds within him virtue's fullness can be compared to an infant: poisonous insects will not sting it; wild animals will not pounce on it; and predatory birds will not swoop down on it. Its bones are soft and its sinews are weak yet its hold is firm. It does not yet know the union of male and female yet its organ rises up; this is the height of seminal essence. It screams all day yet does not become hoarse; this is the height of harmony. To know harmony is called constancy; to know constancy is called enlightened.

LAOZI

The way is broad, it can go to the left as well as to the right.
The ten thousand things depend on it to live and it does not
    refuse them.
It completes its work but does not take credit for it.
It loves and nurtures the ten thousand things and yet does
    not serve as their master.

LAOZI

If you let your mind wander in the bland, merge your spirit in the quiet, flow with things the way they are and have no place for the selfish in it, then all under heaven will be in order.

ZHUANGZI

When the Great Way was in effect, all under heaven was for the common good. They selected the worthy and capable, and they spoke sincerely and cultivated harmony. Therefore, people did not treat only their own relatives as relatives, and did not treat only their own sons as sons. They caused the aged to be able to come to the ends of their lives, the strong to be employed, and the young to be raised. They were compassionate to widows and orphans, childless men and the afflicted, so that all were taken care of. The men had their roles and the women their homes. Merchandise was not cast upon the ground, but did not need to be hoarded for the self; effort was not exerted beyond the person, but did not need to be just for the self. This is why conspiracies did not arise, and why thievery and disorder did not come about. Therefore, the outer doors were not barred. This was called the Great Commonwealth.

RECORD OF RITUAL

Grasping and filling it is not as good as using it. Beating and hammering it, it cannot long be preserved. When gold and jade fill the hall, no one can protect them. To be wealthy and honored and arrogant about it is to bequeath trouble to oneself. When the work is completed and the reputation follows, then for the person to retire is the Way of heaven.

LAOZI

The beginning of the Constant Prior was an undifferentiated void. Empty and homogenous, it was one, constantly one and that is all. Moist and murky, there was not yet light and dark. The spirit was subtle but filled everything; the essence was still and not radiant. Therefore, there was nothing yet that used it, and the ten thousand things were not present. Therefore, there was no form, just a great homogeneity without a name. Heaven could not cover it and the earth could not hold it up. Little, it created the little; big, it created the big, filling everything within the four seas and also enveloping all outside.

MAWANGDUI MANUSCRIPT
"THE ORIGIN OF THE WAY"

After heaven's work has been put in place and heaven's effect has been achieved, the human form is complete and the spirit is born; love, hate, joy, anger, sorrow and happiness are then stored within it. These are called the heavenly emotions.

XUNZI

Heaven's actions have constancy; they do not exist because of the sage Yao nor do they cease because of the tyrant Jie.

XUNZI

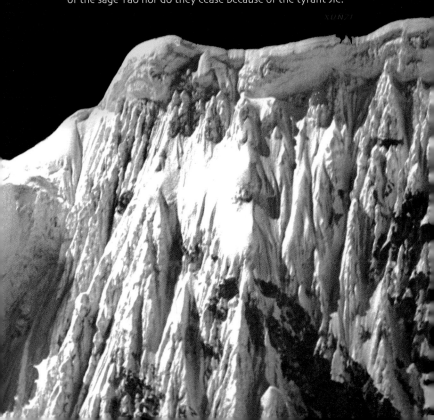

There is a thing formed in murkiness, born before heaven
and earth. Silent and still, it stands alone unchanging,
revolves untangled. It can be the mother of all under
heaven. I do not know its name. Forced to call it something
I call it the Way.

LAOZI

"What do you mean by 'heavenly' and what do you mean
by 'human'?" Mr. Approval from the North Sea said, "Horses
and oxen have four feet, this is what I mean by 'heavenly'.
Putting a halter on the horse's head, piercing the ox's
nose, this is what I mean by 'human'. Therefore, I say, do
not let the human destroy the heavenly; do not let what
is purposeful destroy what is fated; do not die for fame.
Carefully guard it and do not lose it; this is what I mean by
'returning to the true'."

ZHUANGZI

What heaven has commanded is man's inner nature;
what leads the inner nature is the Way; and what cultivates
the way is education. As for the Way, we cannot depart
from it for even an instant. What can be departed from is
not the Way.

DOCTRINE OF THE MEAN

Completing without trying to and finding without seeking is the work of heaven. In this way, no matter how deep man's thoughts are, he doesn't apply them to heaven's work; no matter how great his abilities, he doesn't apply them to it; no matter how keen his examinations, he doesn't apply them to it. This is what is called not contending with heaven's work.

XUNZI

Those who know do not speak; those who speak do not
   know.
Block its openings; shut its door.
Blunt its sharpness; dissolve its anger;
Make harmonious its radiance; make yourself the same as
   its dust.
This is known as the Mysterious Sameness.

LAOZI

The Way of heaven decreases what is excessive and increases what is insufficient. The way of man is not like this; it decreases what is insufficient and raises up what is excessive. Who is able to have more than enough to be able to raise up all under heaven? It is only the Way.

LAOZI

The arrayed stars revolve, the sun and moon shine in turn, the four seasons replace each other, the yin and yang transform, the wind and the rain extend far and wide, and the ten thousand things each come together to give life and each is nurtured to come to completion. We do not see its workings but we do see its effects. This is called divine. Everyone knows that it has come to completion but no one knows its formlessness. This is called the effect of heaven. Only the sage does not seek to know heaven.

XUNZI

We might say by analogy that the Way is to all under heaven as the rivers and seas are to streams and watercourses.

LAOZI

Stars fall and trees call out and the people of the country are all afraid and ask, "What is the cause of this?" I say, "This is nothing at all. It is just the alternations of heaven and earth, the transformations of yin and yang, things that rarely happen. It is alright to regard them as weird, but it is not alright to regard them with awe. There has never been an age that has not occasionally had the sun and moon being eclipsed, the wind and the rain being unseasonable, and weird stars appearing in groups.

XUNZI

Heaven and earth had a beginning: heaven was created through a process of rarification and earth was formed through a process of solidification. The harmonious joining of heaven and earth is the great thread of life. We know of it through the cold and heat, sun and moon, day and night, and explain it in terms of the various shapes and abilities and the different properties. Things join together to create but separate to give life. If you understand joining and creation, separation and life, then heaven and earth are even.

LÜ SHI CHUNQIU

He who treats as upright what is upright does not lose the shape of his inborn nature. Therefore, what are joined together are not webbed toes, and what are forked apart are not extra fingers. What is long is not too much, and what is short is not insufficient. This is why even though a duck's legs are short, to stretch them would make him worry; even though the crane's legs are long, to cut them would make him sad. Therefore, if its nature is to be long it is not to be cut, and if its nature is to be short it is not to be stretched; this will not get rid of worries. Could it be that humaneness and propriety are not man's shape? Those humane men, how many worries they have!

ZHUANGZI

The emperor of the South Sea was Minnow, the emperor of the North Sea was Daft, and the emperor of the central region was Dumpling. Minnow and Daft occasionally met each other in the land of Dumpling, and Dumpling treated them very well. Minnow and Daft planned a way to repay his kindness, saying, "Men all have seven openings to see, hear, eat, and breathe. This one alone doesn't have any. Let's trying boring him some!" Every day they bored one hole. On the seventh day Dumpling died.

ZHUANGZI

Exhausting your spirit to make everything one while not knowing that they are the same is what I call "three in the morning." What do I mean by "three in the morning"? When the monkey trainer was handing out acorns, he said, "You get three in the morning and four in the evening." The pack of monkeys were all angry. So he said, "OK, four in the morning and three in the evening." The pack of monkeys were all delighted. The substance of the words hadn't changed and yet they brought about happiness and anger, just because of this. This is why the sage harmonizes them with right and wrong and rests in the heavenly balance. This is what I call walking the two roads.

ZHUANGZI

If we have to use a curve and plumb line, compass and square to make something square, this is to scrape away its inborn nature; if we have to use rope and knots, glue and lacquer to make something sturdy, this is to invade its virtue. As for the crouchings and bendings of rites and music, the smiles and fawning of humaneness and propriety used to comfort the hearts of all under heaven, these lose their constant state.

ZHUANGZI

Master Dongguo asked Zhuangzi, "This thing called the
   Way, where is it?"
Zhuangzi said, "There's no place it isn't."
Master Dongguo said, "You have to do better than that!"
Zhuangzi said, "It's in an ant."
"How could it be so low as that?"
"It's in the scrub grass."
"How could it be lower still!"
"It's in the tiles and shards."
"How could it be lower still!"
"It's in the shit and piss!"
Master Dongguo did not respond.

ZHUANGZI

The True Man of antiquity did not know of loving life, did
not know of hating death. He came out without tearing; he
went in without refusing. He went briskly, he came briskly,
and that was all. He didn't forget where he began; he didn't
seek where he would end. He received and took pleasure in
it, and then forgot about it and returned it. This is what I
call not using the mind to decrease the Way, not using man
to help heaven. This is what I call the True Man.

ZHUANGZI

Zhuangzi was wandering around in the park at Carved Mound when he saw a strange magpie that came flying from the southern regions. Its wings were seven feet wide and its eyes were an inch in diameter. It brushed against Zhuangzi's forehead and then roosted in a grove of chestnut trees. Zhuangzi said, "What kind of bird is this! Its wings are enormous but it doesn't go anywhere; its eyes are huge but it can't see where it's going!" Then he hitched up his robe, strode forward, held his crossbow firm and waited for it. Just then, he saw a cicada that had found a lovely spot of shade and had forgotten itself. A praying mantis was grabbing the cicada's wings and snatching it, but looking at what it was getting it too forgot its own form. The strange magpie was following it, ready to pluck the praying mantis. However, it too, seeing what it was getting, had forgotten its true self. Zhuangzi was startled and said, "Ah! Things really pile up on top of each other, two different species inviting each other." He threw down his crossbow and turned around and ran off, just as the game warden was chasing him and shouting at him. Zhuangzi returned home and for three days did not come out of his room.

ZHUANGZI

You forget your feet with the shoes fitting. You forget your waist with the belt fitting. Knowledge forgets right and wrong with the mind fitting. You have no change inside, no following outside, with the convergence of affairs fitting. You begin with what is fitting and never experience what is not fitting with the fitting of forgetting what is fitting.

ZHUANGZI

The one-legged Kui said to the millipede, "I use one leg to hop and move, and I think nothing of it. Now how do you manage to get all those ten thousand legs of yours to work?" The millipede said, "It's not like that. Haven't you seen a man spit? *Hyuck*, and then the big ones are like pearls and the little ones mist, all mixed up and coming down such that you can never count them. Now I just move my heavenly mechanism and don't know how it is."

ZHUANGZI

The life of things is a gallop, a rush, never a movement and not changing, never a moment and not shifting. What to do, what not to do? It is certain that things will transform of themselves.

ZHUANGZI

Government

In antiquity, when the people were first born and there were still no laws or government, it was described as "people having different senses of propriety." In this way, one person had one sense of propriety, while two people had two senses of propriety, and ten people had ten senses of propriety. The more numerous people became, what they called propriety also became more numerous. In this way, people approved of their own sense of propriety and denied the sense of propriety of others; therefore, they denied each other. In this way, within families among fathers and sons, older and younger brothers, there arose resentment and hatred, and they split up and were not able to live in accord. Under heaven people all used water and fire and even poison to hurt each other, coming to the point that those with extra strength could not work for others and those with rotting excess goods would not share them, while hermits with fine ways would not teach them to others. The chaos under heaven was like that of the birds and the beasts. Those who understood that the chaos of the world came from there not being governors and elders chose the most worthy and capable under heaven and put him in place as the son of heaven. When the son of heaven was in place, because his strength was still insufficient, they again chose the most worthy and capable in the world and set them up

as the three ministers. After the son of heaven and the three
ministers were in place, since the world was so big and broad
and the people of distant kingdoms and different lands
had different senses of right and wrong, benefit and harm,
and they couldn't know each and every one of them, they
divided up the ten-thousand kingdoms and put lords and
rulers in place. Once the lords and rulers were in place, since
their strength was still insufficient, they again selected the
most worthy and capable in the kingdom and set them up to
be governors and elders.

When grasses and trees are flowering and growing, axes are not to enter into the forests to shorten their life and cut off their growth. When turtles and fishes are breeding and hatching, nets and poisons are not to enter the marshes to shorten their life and cut off their growth. In the spring one plows, in the summer weeds, in the autumn harvests, and in the winter stores. If these four activities do not lose their seasons, then the five grains will not be cut off and the common people will have more than enough to eat. One dredges the ponds and bays and rivers and streams. If one is careful about the seasonal prohibitions, then the fish will be plentiful and the common people will have more than enough to use. If the felling of trees is not out of season, then the mountains and forests will mature and the common people will have more than enough resources. These are the actions of a sage king.

XUNZI

The wise ruler is like the torso, his ministers like his arms; the ruler like a shout, his ministers like an echo. The ruler plants the root, and the ministers trim the branches; the ruler controls the essentials, and the ministers put the details into action.

SHEN BUHAI

The ruler does not show what he wants, for if he shows what he wants his ministers will naturally polish the apple in that direction. The ruler does not show his intentions, for if he shows his intentions his ministers will naturally display themselves differently.

HAN FEIZI

You can have many wise people, but you cannot have many rulers. You can be without wise people, but you cannot be without a ruler.

SHEN DAO

The reason a ruler is honored is because he commands. If his commands are not put into effect, it is the same as not having a ruler. Therefore, the ruler is careful about commands.

SHEN BUHAI

The way ministers usurp the privileges of the ruler is like the way the landscape takes shape, moving little by little; this causes the ruler to lose his bearings, such that east and west change faces and he doesn't even know it.

HAN FEIZI

The more taboos there are in the world, the poorer the
   people are.
The more sharp tools the people have, the more benighted
   the country is.
The more clever crafts the people have, the more fantastic
   goods arise.
The more prominent fancy things become, the more thieves
   and robbers there are.

LAOZI

Not honoring the worthy causes the people not to contend.
Not valuing goods which are hard to come by causes the
   people not to steal.
Not showing what you want causes their hearts to be
   undisturbed.

LAOZI

Confucius said: "Lead them with government and regulate
them with punishments and the people will stay out of
the way but be without a sense of shame. Lead them with
virtue and regulate them with the rites and the people will
have a sense of shame and moreover will go out of their
way to serve."

ANALECTS

Only he who has nothing to do with ruling all under heaven can be entrusted with all under heaven.

ZHUANGZI

The losing of a kingdom is never the fault of a single man, and the putting of a kingdom in order is never the result of a single man.

SHEN DAO

Fire and water have vapor but are without life, grass and trees have life but are without knowledge, birds and beasts have knowledge but are without propriety. Man has vapor, has life, has knowledge and moreover also has propriety, and thus is most honored under heaven. His power is not like that of an ox, his running is not like that of a horse, and yet he puts oxen and horses to use. Why is this? I say: Men are able to form groups, while those are not able to form groups. How is it that men are able to form groups? I say: By division. How can division work? I say: By propriety. Therefore, if one divides according to propriety there is harmony, if there is harmony there is unity, if there is unity there will be much strength, and if there is much strength they will be strong, and if they are strong they will be able to overcome things.

As for the government of the bright king, the achievements cover all under heaven and yet seem not to be his own, while the transformations extend to all the ten thousand things and yet the people do not depend on him. There is no one who praises his name, he just lets things be happy of themselves. He is one who takes his stand in the unfathomable and wanders where there is nothing at all.

ZHUANGZI

Mencius said to King Xuan of Qi, "How would it be if one of your subjects entrusted his wife and children to his friend and went traveling to Chu, and when he returned found that his wife and children had frozen and starved?" The king said, "I would dump him as a friend." "How about if the Master of the Guard was unable to control his men?" "Cut him off." "And how about if there is disorder within the borders of the state?" The king turned to the others around him and changed the subject.

MENCIUS

There have been cases where one who was not humane has gotten a state, but there has never been a case where one who was not humane has all under heaven.

MENCIUS

Ji Kangzi asked Confucius about government saying: "How would it be to kill the unjust in order to make way for the just?" Confucius replied saying: "In your doing government, what is the use of killing? If you desire the good, your people will be good. The virtue of the gentleman is the wind, while that of the inferior man is the grass. With the wind on the grass, it necessarily bends."

ANALECTS

There have been cases in which there are good laws and yet disorder, but from antiquity to the present I have never heard of a case of there being a gentleman in charge of government and yet disorder. When tradition says "Order is born from the gentleman and disorder is born from the petty person," this is what it means.

XUNZI

One who steals a belt buckle is executed, while one who steals a state is made a lord.

ZHUANGZI

Elevating the worthy is the basis of government.

MOZI

The reason why the rivers and the seas are able to be king of all the watercourses is that they are good at putting themselves beneath the others and therefore they are able to be king of all the watercourses. This is why the sage wishing to be over others necessarily puts himself beneath them with his words, wishing to be ahead of others necessarily puts his person behind them. This is why the sage occupies the top place but the people don't regard him as heavy, why he occupies the front but the people are not hurt by it. This is why all under heaven enjoy pushing him forward and do not feel oppressed. Because of his not contending, therefore under heaven no one contends with him.

LAOZI

The alternations of hot and cold are not transformed by a single spark. The affairs under heaven cannot all be known by a single man. The vastness of the sea's waters are not fed by the flow of a single river. This is why in ruling the world the wise ruler hurries to seek out others and does not do it alone.

HE GUANZI

King Hui of Liang said, "I would like to receive instruction from you." Mencius replied, "Is there any difference between killing a man with a club or a sword?" The king said, "There is no difference at all." "Is there any difference between a sword or bad government?" "There is no difference at all." Mencius said, "There is fatty meat in your kitchens and fat horses in your stables, while there are starved looks on your people and starved corpses in the wastelands. This is tantamount to leading animals and eating people. People even detest it when animals eat other animals. To be the father and mother of the people but in running the government not to be able to avoid leading animals and eating people, how do you find your place as the father and mother of the people?"

MENCIUS

Now if I am to adopt a policy that seeks to give benefit to all under heaven, it will be universality. In this way, those with good eyes and ears will do the looking and hearing for others, those with strong arms and legs will act and move for others, and those with the way will teach and instruct others. In this way, those who are aged and without wives and sons will be cared for to the end of their days, and the disabled and orphaned will have support to grow up.

MOZI

Qinzi asked Yang Zhu: "If you could get rid of a single hair to help the whole world, would you do it?" Yang Zhu said: "The world certainly couldn't be helped by a single hair." Qinzi said: "But if it could be, would you do it?" Yang Zhu didn't respond. Qinzi went out and spoke with Mengsun Yang, who said: "You didn't get my master's meaning. Let me explain it to you. If you could get 10,000 dollars for slicing off some of your skin, would you do it?" He said: "I would." Mengsun Yang said: "If you could get an entire kingdom by cutting off one of your limbs, would you do it?" Qinzi was silent for awhile. Mengsun Yang said: "It is clear that a hair is less than skin, and skin is less than a limb. However, adding up hair you get the skin, and adding up skin you get a limb. Though one hair is certainly just a tenth of one percent of an entire body, how could you treat it lightly?

LIEZI

In the kingdom of an enlightened ruler, there is no literature in books—they take the law as their teaching; there are no sayings of the past kings—they take their deputies as the teachers; there are no private weapons—they regard killing in battle as bravery. In this way, the speech of the people will certainly follow the law, their actions will certainly be productive, and their bravery will stay within the army.

HAN FEIZI

Prune your trees from time to time, not letting the branches get big and the trunks small, for if the branches are big and the trunks small they will not be able to stand up to the spring winds, and if they don't stand up to the spring winds the branches will harm the flowers. If the princes are multitudinous, the royal house will be beset with worries. The way to stop them is to prune your trees from time to time, not letting the branches get too luxuriant. If the trees are pruned from time to time, parties and cliques will be disbanded.

HAN FEIZI

There was a man of Song who was plowing a field, in the middle of which there was a tree stump. A rabbit came running, crashed into the tree stump and broke its neck and died. With that the farmer put down his plow and waited by the stump, looking forward to getting more rabbits. Not only was he not able to get any more rabbits, but instead became the laughing-stock of the kingdom of Song. Now all those who want to use the government of the past kings to rule the people of the present age are of the sort who wait by the stump.

HAN FEIZI

If the horses are frightened by the cart, then the gentleman will not be safe in the cart. If the common people are frightened of the government, then the gentleman will not be safe in power. If the horses are frightened of the cart, there is nothing better than calming them. If the common people are frightened of the government, there is nothing better than being kind to them.

XUNZI

The way of the enlightened ruler is to cause the intelligent to present all of their deliberations and for the ruler to decide affairs based on them; thus, the ruler's intelligence will not be exhausted. It is to cause the worthy to make use of their talents and for the ruler to employ them based on them; thus, the ruler's abilities will not be exhausted.

HAN FEIZI

If you were to make the ruler the most knowledgeable, then the ruler alone would be responsible for everything under heaven and would be belabored; being belabored he would be exhausted, being exhausted he would decline, and being in decline he would revert to the way of not being responsible.

SHEN DAO

Past ages did not have the same teachings; which past should we take as a model? The emperors and kings did not duplicate each other; which rituals should we follow? Rituals and laws are settled according to the times, rules and regulations each follow what is appropriate, weapons and tools all have their uses. This is why I say "There is not a single way to rule the world, and in enriching the state one does not need to take the past as a model."

SHANG JUN SHU

There are five obstructions for the ruler of men: when ministers shut out their ruler, when ministers regulate resources and profit, when ministers independently put commands into effect, when ministers put their own ideas into effect, and when ministers plant their own men.

HAN FEIZI

Someone said to Confucius, "Why don't you do something in government?" Confucius answered him: "The *Documents* say: 'To be filial to your elders and friendly with your siblings is to act in government.' This is also to do something in government. What do I have to do with doing something in government!"

ANALECTS

A skillful carpenter can cut a straight line with his eye alone, but he necessarily first uses a rule and compass to take his measurements. The wisest person can take care of business on his own, but necessarily uses the models of the past kings for comparison. Therefore, if the plumb line is straight, warped wood can be planed; if the level is true, high knots can be shaved off; if the balance is suspended, what is too light can be made heavier; and if measures are set out, what is too few can be made more plentiful. Therefore, use the law to govern the state, just letting it run its course.

HAN FEIZI

Three generations in a row the people of Yue assassinated their ruler. Prince Sou, worried about this, fled to the Cinnabar Cave, and the state of Yue was left without a ruler. Searching for Prince Sou unsuccessfully, the people of Yue followed him to the Cinnabar Cave, but Prince Sou was unwilling to come out. They smoked him out and put him on the royal chariot. As Prince Sou grasped the railing to step up into the chariot, he looked up to heaven and cried out, "A ruler! A ruler! Is it only impossible to spare me from this?" It was not that Prince Sou hated being a ruler; he hated the worries of being a ruler. Prince Sou can be said to be one who did not let the kingdom injure his life. This is exactly why the people of Yue wanted to get him to be their ruler.

ZHUANGZI

King Ling of Chu loved slender waists. In his kingdom there were many starving people on diets.

HAN FEIZI

Formerly, Lord Zhao of Han got drunk and fell asleep. The Guardian of the Hat saw that the ruler was cold and covered him with a coat. When the lord woke up, he was happy, asking those around him, "Who covered me with the coat?" They said, "The Guardian of the Hat." The ruler thereupon punished both the Guardian of the Coat and the Guardian of the Hat. He punished the Guardian of the Coat for having failed in his service, and the Guardian of the Hat for having overstepped his responsibility. It was not that he didn't dislike being cold, but he regarded the danger of usurping offices to be even greater than that of the cold.

HAN FEIZI

If he values using his own body more than managing all under heaven, then all under heaven can be consigned to him. If he is more careful with his own body than with managing all under heaven, then all under heaven can be entrusted to him.

ZHUANGZI

Confucius said: "Governing with virtue is like the North Star occupying its place while all the other stars are under it holding it up."

ANALECTS

Zhuangzi was fishing along the Pu River. The king of Chu sent two officers to go and announce to him: "I would like to trouble you with all within our borders." Zhuangzi clutched the fishing pole and, without turning around, said, "I hear that Chu has a holy turtle that has already been dead for three thousand years. The king keeps it wrapped in cloth and boxed, and stores it up in the ancestral temple. Would this turtle rather be dead with its bones left behind and honored, or would it rather be alive and dragging its tail in the mud?" The two officers said, "It would rather be alive and dragging its tail in the mud." Zhuangzi said, "Go away! I'm going to drag my tail in the mud!"

ZHUANGZI

One moving through water marks the deep places; if the marks are not clear then others will fall in. One governing the people marks the Way; if the marks are not clear then there will be disorder.

XUNZI

The way of ruling is to cause ministers necessarily to be responsible for what they say, but also to be responsible for what they do not say.

HAN FEIZI

The way of the ruling is to govern what is near and not what is distant, to govern what is clear and not what is murky, to govern the one and not the two. If the ruler is able to govern what is near, then what is distant will be in order; if the ruler is able to govern what is clear, then what is murky will be transformed; and if the ruler is able to confront the one, then the hundred affairs will all be correct. By comprehensively listening to everything under heaven, there will be more than enough days and you govern what is insufficient; this is the height of governing. If you are already able to govern what is near, and you still strive to govern what is distant; if you are already able to govern what is clear, and you still strive to govern what is murky; and if you are already able to confront the one, and you still strive to correct the hundred, this is to go too far; going too far is just the same as not doing enough.

XUNZI

The wise ruler's governing a kingdom is like a three-inch hinge; when it moves, the whole world is settled. It is like the core of the foundation; when it is true, the whole world is well ordered. When a single saying is correct, then the world is upright; when a single saying is askew, then the world comes to naught.

SHEN BUHAI

The *Changes* says, "The haughty dragon; there is regret."
Confucius said, "This speaks of being above and treating
those below arrogantly; there has never been a case of one
who treats those below arrogantly not being in danger.
As for the sage's establishment of government, it is like
climbing a tree: the higher one gets, the more one fears
what is below. Therefore it says, 'The haughty dragon;
there is regret.'"

Zi Gong asked about government. Confucius said: "Enough food, enough weapons and the trust of the people." Zi Gong said, "If you had to give up something, of these three which would be first?" The Master said: "Give up the weapons." Zi Gong said, "If you had to give up something, of these two what would be first?" The Master said, "Give up the food. From ancient times, there has always been death, but a people without trust will not stand."

ANALECTS

From what does ritual arise? When people are born they have desires. When they cannot get what they desire, then they cannot be without seeking, and seeking without limits, then there cannot not be contention, with contention then disorder, and with disorder then poverty. The prior kings hated this disorder, and therefore regulated rituals in order to divide things, in order to satisfy people's desires, and in order to provide what people seek.

XUNZI

Confucius said: "If one governs his own person, what problem does he have with serving in government? If one cannot govern his own person, how can he govern others?"

ANALECTS

The world is not any one person's world; it is the world's world. The harmony of the yin and yang does not cause just one species to grow. The sweet dew and the timely rain do not favor any one thing, and the ruler of the ten thousand people does not favor any one person.

LÜ SHI CHUNQIU

When a single minister monopolizes a ruler, the other ministers are all overshadowed and can easily destroy the kingdom. This is why the wise ruler causes all of the ministers to work together like the spokes of a wheel, and doesn't allow any to monopolize the ruler.

SHEN BUHAI

The rule of the sage is this: Empty their hearts and fill their bellies, weaken their wills and strengthen their bones. If you constantly cause the people to be without knowledge and without desires, and cause the knowledgeable not to dare to act, then there will not be any who are unruly.

LAOZI

Governing a large state is like cooking a small fish.

LAOZI

Sagehood

Heaven and earth give birth to the gentleman and the gentleman brings order to heaven and earth. The gentleman is the third part of heaven and earth, the main support of the ten thousand things, the father and mother of the people.

XUNZI

The Master said: "Some plain food to eat and water to drink, a bent arm for a pillow: happiness is also to be found in its midst. To be rich and honored improperly is to me as if floating clouds."

ANALECTS

Humaneness is being human. To join them together and to put it into words is the Way.

MENCIUS

Gaozi said, "Human nature is like swirling water. If you open it to the east it will flow east, if you open it to the west it will flow west. Human nature's not being divided between good and not good is just like water's not being divided between east and west." Mencius said, "It is true that water makes no distinction between east and west, but does it make no distinction between high and low? Human nature's being good is just like water's going down. There are no men who are not good, just as there is no water that does not flow down. Now, with water you can slap it, and cause it to leap up over your forehead, or pump it and make it go up a mountain, but can it be that this is the nature of water? It is the force that causes it to be so. That man can be made to be not good, his nature is just the same as this."

MENCIUS

People all have things that they will not bear. To extend this to what they will bear is humaneness. People all have things that they will not do. To extend this to what they will do is propriety. If people can fill out the heart that does not desire to harm others, they will have more humaneness than they could ever use. If people can fill out the heart that will not overstep the bounds, they will have more propriety than they could ever use.

MENCIUS

One such as this will store the gold in the mountains, store the pearls in the depths, will not regard goods and riches as profitable, will not draw near to fame and wealth, will not take joy in a long life nor bemoan an early death, and will not luxuriate in getting ahead nor feel ashamed at being impoverished. He will not snatch the profits of a whole generation to be his private share; he will not regard ruling all under heaven as his own place of eminence. Eminent he is bright, taking the ten thousand things as a single storehouse, regarding life and death as being the same condition.

ZHUANGZI

A lame turtle can go a thousand miles, but a team of six thoroughbreds, one going forward, one going backward, one going to the left, one going to the right, will not get anywhere. How could the differences between people's talents and natures be anything like that between a lame turtle and a team of six thoroughbreds. And yet that the lame turtle gets there and the six thoroughbreds do not is due to no other reason than that one works at it and the other doesn't. Even though the road be near, if you don't walk it you won't get there. Even though affairs be small, if you don't do them you won't succeed.

XUNZI

Sima Niu asked about the gentleperson. Confucius said, "The gentleperson is unconcerned and unafraid." Niu said, "Unconcerned and unafraid, is this all there is to being a gentleperson?" Confucius said, "If you reflect within yourself and find nothing to be ashamed of, how could you be concerned or afraid?"

ANALECTS

Confucius said, "Only the humane person is able to love others and is able to disdain others."

ANALECTS

Confucius said, "The gentleperson looks for it in himself; the petty person looks for it in others."

ANALECTS

Confucius said, "The gentleperson desires to be hesitant in speech, but diligent in action."

ANALECTS

Confucius said, "When I was fifteen I set my heart on learning; at thirty I took my stand; at forty I was not confused; at fifty I knew the mandate of heaven; at sixty my ear was obedient; at seventy I could follow my heart's desire without stepping over the line.

ANALECTS

Confucius said, "I don't worry about being without position; I worry about how to establish it. I don't worry about no one knowing me; I seek to be worth knowing."

ANALECTS

Confucius said, "The gentleperson is harmonious but does not copy. The petty person copies but is not harmonious."

ANALECTS

Confucius said, "The gentleperson is unruffled. The petty person is uptight."

ANALECTS

Confucius said, "Only the wisest and the most foolish do not change."

ANALECTS

I'm going to tell you about it recklessly; listen to it recklessly.
Who carries the sun and moon on his shoulders and tucks
the universe under his arms, joins right together with them
and leaves the muddle behind, regarding slaves as exalted?
The mass of men struggle and strain, but the sage is stupid
and dull, partaking in ten thousand years and blending them
all into one. The ten thousand things are complete in him
and he takes them as enveloping each other.

ZHUANGZI

If your heart is at peace then even beauty that does not come up to the average will be able to nurture the eye, sounds that do not come up to the average will be able to nurture the ears, vegetables and a soup of boiled greens will be able to nurture the mouth, and clothes of coarse cloth and sandals of coarse hemp will be able to nurture the body. A snug room, rush blinds, a straw carpet, and a beat-up table will be able to nurture one's form. Therefore, even if one doesn't have any of the beauties of the ten thousand things he can still nurture his enjoyment, and even if one is not placed among the ranked still he can nurture his reputation. If you were to give all under heaven to one such as this he would do much for the world and little for his selfish enjoyment. This is what is called taking the self seriously and making other things work for you.

XUNZI

If you treat the aged as they should be treated then those in the prime of life will be with you; if you are not hard on those suffering hardship then the successful will join you; if you act behind the curtains and give without seeking to be repaid, then the worthy and unworthy alike will be one with you. If someone has these three ways of conduct, even if she makes a great mistake, how could heaven not accord with her!

XUNZI

The gentleperson acts according to his natural place, not longing for what is outside of it. If he is naturally wealthy and honored, he acts within wealth and honor; if he is naturally poor and of low status, he acts within poverty and low status. If he is naturally among the barbarians, he acts among the barbarians. If he is naturally in turmoil and difficulty, he acts within turmoil and difficulty. There is nowhere that the gentleperson goes that he is not self possessed. In high position, he does not bully those below. In low position he does not suck up to those above. He makes himself correct and does not seek from others, and then there is no resentment. Above he does not resent heaven and below he does not blame others.

DOCTRINE OF THE MEAN

The sage knows the turmoil of the techniques of the mind and sees the troubles of obsession. Therefore, he is without desires, without hatred, without beginning, without end, without near, without distant, without broad, without shallow, without ancient, without recent, but impartially arranges all the ten thousand things and weighs them evenly in the balance. This is why the multitude of differences cannot block each other and disorder his thought processes.

XUNZI

Without going out the door, one knows all under heaven.
Without looking out the window, one sees the way of
   heaven.
The further one goes out, the nearer one knows.
This is why the sage does not move and yet knows, does not
   look and yet names, does not strive and yet completes.

LAOZI

The petty man can become a gentleman but does not want to become a gentleman. The gentleman can become a petty man but does not want to become a petty man. The petty man and the gentleman have never not been able to become each other; that they do not become each other is because they cannot be made to. Therefore, it is true that the man of the street can become the sage Yu, but it is not necessarily the case that he will be able to become Yu.

XUNZI

Your name or your body, which is more intimate?
Your body or your goods, which is more abundant?
Gain or loss, which is more painful?
This is why stinginess necessarily incurs great expense,
Having much stored away necessarily leads to great loss.
Therefore, know satisfaction and you will not be disgraced;
Know when to stop and you will not be in danger, and will
    be able to long endure.

LAOZI

As for the inner-nature of the sage and the inner-nature of the middling man, at their birth they were not yet different.

GUODIAN MANUSCRIPT,
"CHENG'S HEARING OF IT"

You have only appropriated the shape of a man and are delighted by it. But the shape of man goes through ten thousand transformations that never begin to have an ultimate shape. Can you count all of the ways that it brings joy! Therefore, the sage wanders where things don't get to follow and all exist. He looks well on early death as he does on old age; he looks well on the beginning as on the end. Other men can only imitate him; how much more so that which is tied to the ten thousand things, and which awaits the one transformation!

ZHUANGZI

Among the men of Chu there was one who lost his bow, but did not wish to search for it, saying "A man of Chu lost it and a man of Chu will get it; why would I search for it?" Confucius heard of this and said, "Omit 'Chu' and it would be acceptable." Lao Dan heard of it and said, "Omit 'man' and it would be acceptable. This is how Lao Dan was perfectly impartial.

LÜ SHI CHUNQIU

The gentleman makes use of things; the petty man is used by things.

XUNZI

The sage embraces the One and is a model for all under heaven, does not show off and so is bright, does not consider himself right and so is manifest, does not brag and so has success, is not arrogant and so is long-lasting. It is because he does not contend that no one under heaven can contend with him.

LAOZI

Zi Gong said, "If there were one who gave widely to the people and was able to help the masses, how would that be? Could you call that being humane?" Confucius said: "How would it be just a matter of humaneness; if need be, it would be sagely. Even Yao and Shun would be deficient in comparison to him. As for humaneness, oneself wishing to be established, one establishes others; oneself wishing to succeed, one causes others to succeed. Being able to take analogies from near at hand can be called the recipe for humaneness."

ANALECTS

Zengzi said, "Having ability and inquiring after those unable, having much and inquiring after those with little; having but seeming to be without, being solid but seeming to be empty, being crossed and yet not cross, in the old days my friend acted like this."

ANALECTS

The gentleman regards lightly those who take perception to be the analysis of phrases and discrimination to be talking about things, as well as those of broad learning who insist on their way and do not accord with the regulations of the king.

XUNZI

The *Poetry* says, "Over brocaded robes a plain dress," the sign of disdaining elegance. Therefore, the way of the gentleperson is to conceal oneself and yet day by day to be revealed. The way of the petty person is to show off and yet day by day to be diminished. The way of the gentleperson is to be plain tasting and not too spicy, simple and not elegant, warm and yet ordered. Knowing the nearness of the distant, knowing the source of suasion, knowing the appearance of the minute, you can enter into virtue with him.

DOCTRINE OF THE MEAN

The Duke of She asked Zi Lu about Confucius. Zi Lu didn't respond. The Master said, "Why didn't you just say something like that as a person he gets so excited that he forgets to eat, in his joy he forgets his concerns, and doesn't know that old age is about to arrive?"

ANALECTS

The gentleperson is careful about what he does not see, apprehensive about what he does not hear. Nothing is more visible than the obscure, nothing more apparent than the tiny. Therefore, the gentleperson is careful about his solitude.

DOCTRINE OF THE MEAN

A good farmer does not stop plowing on account of floods and drought, a good merchant does not stop trading on account of losses and taxes, and a real gentleman is not neglectful of the Way on account of poverty and hardship.

XUNZI

There was once a man of Song who, concerned that the seedlings in his field were not growing, tugged at them. He returned home exhausted and told his family, "Today I'm beat; I've been helping the seedlings to grow." His son rushed off to look at them, and the seedlings were withered. There are few in the world who do not "help their seedlings to grow." There are those who feel that there's no use and just give up, those who do not "weed." But the ones who help them to grow, who tug on the seedlings, not only do they not help them, instead they harm them!

MENCIUS

Categories ought not to be differentiated. Therefore, the wise person selects one of them and unifies things in it. The farmer is well versed in the fields, but cannot become the master of agriculture; the merchant is well versed in the markets, but cannot become the master of the markets; and the craftsman is well versed in tools, but cannot become the master of tools. There are people who are incapable of these three skills and yet can rule the three occupations. These are those who are well versed in the Way, but not well versed in things. Those who are well versed in things treat individual things as individual things, but those who are well versed in the Way treat all things impartially. Therefore, the gentleman, being united with the Way, uses it to examine things; being united with the Way, he is correct and his examination of things is perceptive; and, with an upright will motivating his perceptions, then the ten thousand things are all his organs.

XUNZI

If you are respectful in your bearing and loyal in your heart, deal with others with the rites and propriety and treat them with compassion, then you may travel anywhere under heaven and even if you are caught up with barbarians there will be no one who will not honor you.

XUNZI

Heaven does not stop winter on account of men hating the cold, the earth does not stop being broad on account of men hating long distances, and the gentleman does not stop acting on account of petty men's carping. Heaven has its constant way, earth has its constant number, and the gentleman has his constant bearing. The gentleman follows his constancy while the petty man calculates his achievements.

XUNZI

If now we cause the man of the street to submerse himself in study and focus his mind on one intent, and think and examine things through thoroughly, day after day for a long time, accumulating goodness without cease, then he will break through to divine brightness and form a triad with heaven and earth.

XUNZI

One who regards wealth as right cannot yield his salary; one who regards eminence as right cannot yield his fame; one who has a taste for power cannot give the handle to others. Holding onto these things, they are cold; letting them go, they are sorrowful. And never once do they have a moment of reflection to notice that this is why they never get any rest. This is heaven's punishment of the people.

ZHUANGZI

Lord Yuan of Song was about to have some pictures painted, and the crowd of scribes all arrived, received their canvases and took their places, licking their brushes and ink, half of them outside the room. There was one scribe who arrived late, sauntered in, received his canvas but did not take a place, and instead went to his room. The ruler sent someone to see what he was doing, and found that he had taken off his clothes and was humming away naked. The lord said, "He will do, this is a true artist!"

ZHUANGZI

Zi Gong asked about the gentleperson. The Master said: "First she practices what she preaches and afterwards she follows it."

ANALECTS

The sage does not hoard. Having strived on behalf of others, he himself has ever more; having given to others, he himself is ever richer.

LAOZI

Zi Si said, "Wealth and honor are very easy for me to achieve and yet it seems that other people are unable to achieve them. Not to take from others is what I called wealth; not to take offense at the acts of others is what I call honor. To do these two things means that wealth and honor are at hand."

KONG CONGZI

One who knows others is knowledgeable; one who knows
   herself is bright.
One who defeats others is powerful; one who overcomes
   herself is stronger.
Knowing satisfaction is to be rich.

LAOZI

Only after there are things that a man will not do can he do great things.

MENCIUS

The gentleman respects that which resides within himself and does not long for that which resides with heaven.

XUNZI

Death

The Great Clod transports me with a form, labors me
with life, eases me with old age, and rests me with death.
Therefore, thinking well of my life, for the same reason
I think well of my death.

ZHUANGZI

Ji Lu asked about serving the ghosts and spirits. The Master
said, "If you are not yet able to serve men, how will you be
able to serve the ghosts and spirits?" Lu said, "Dare I ask
about death?" He said, "If you do not yet know about life,
how will you know about death?"

ANALECTS

The suppleness of man's life becomes rigid with his death.
The pliability of the ten thousand things and the grasses and
    trees becomes brittle with their death.
Therefore, rigidity is the disciple of death, while suppleness
    is the disciple of life.
This is why when weapons are hard they are not victorious
    and when a tree is strong it is cut down.
Therefore, the rigid occupy the lower place while the supple
    occupy the higher place.

LAOZI

The widowed Queen Xuan of Qin was in love with Wei Chou. The queen was sick and about to die, and issued an order saying, "When you bury me, you must bury Master Wei along with me." Wei was concerned about this. One Yong Rui spoke to the queen on behalf of Wei saying, "Do you think that the dead have knowledge?" The queen said, "They do not." To which he said, "If your divine spirit clearly knows that the dead are without any knowledge, why would you emptily have one loved in life buried with an unknowing dead person! On the other hand, if the dead do have knowledge, your deceased husband the late king will have been piling up anger at you for a long time now, and you will be so busy trying to make excuses for your faults that you'll have no time to fool around with Wei Chou." The queen said, "Very well," and then she stopped.

STRATEGIES OF THE WARRING STATES

Everything that lives between heaven and earth must die; death is something that men cannot avoid. It is part of nature that filial children's respect for their parents and caring parents' love for their children is felt in their flesh and bones. When those who you respect and who you love die, human nature would not be able to bear discarding them in a ditch. This is why we have funerals.

LÜ SHI CHUNQIU

Duke Jing of Qi had a thousand teams of horses, but on the day he died the people had nothing to praise him about. Bo Yi and Shu Qi starved to death at the foot of Mount Shouyang, and the people praise them until today. What meaning is there in this?

ANALECTS

Some deaths are heavier than Mount Tai, while others are lighter than a goose feather.

RECORDS OF THE GRAND HISTORIAN

The Master said, "Hearing the Way in the morning, dying that evening would be fine."

ANALECTS

Mourning rites have nothing in them but to illustrate
the propriety of life and death, to send off the dead with
mournful respect, and at last to store them away. In burial,
one respectfully stores away the human form. In sacrificing,
one respectfully serves its spirit. With monuments, eulogies,
and genealogies one respectfully passes on their name. In
serving the living, one ornaments the beginning. In sending
off the dead, one ornaments the end. When the beginning
and end are both provided for, then the service of the filial
son is finished and the way of the sage is complete.

XUNZI

In the funeral rites, one decorates the dead with the things
of the living, sending them off with the great symbols of
their life. In this way, one serves the dead as though they
are living, and serves the departed as though they are
present, uniting the end and beginning.

XUNZI

When Yan Yuan died, the Master wept inconsolably.
His followers said, "Master, you are certainly inconsolable!"
He said, "Am I inconsolable? If I were not inconsolable about
this person, then for whom would I ever be!"

ANALECTS

What the ten thousand things differ in is life; what they have in common is death. In life there are the worthy and the foolish, the honored and the debased; these are what are different. In death there is corruption and decay; these are what are the same. Nevertheless, worth and foolishness, honor and debasement are not what they are capable of, just as corruption and decay are also not what they are capable of. Therefore, life is not what gives life and death is not what kills; worth is not what makes the worthy and foolishness is not what makes the foolish; and honor is not what makes the honored and debasement is not what makes the debased. And yet the ten thousand things are the same in living and the same in dying, are the same in worth and foolishness, the same in honor and debasement. To die at the age of ten is to die, and to die at a hundred is also to die. Humane sages die just as do terrible fools. In life they were the sages Yao and Shun, but in death they are rotten bones; in life they were the tyrants Jie and Zhou, but in death they are rotten bones. The rotten bones are the same; who could tell the difference between them! Always rushing after life, who has time for what comes after death?

LIEZI

Master Mozi said, "This is what I call making their behavior convenient and making their customs proper. Formerly, in the eastern part of Yue there was the state of Kaimo. When an eldest son was born they cut him up and ate him, saying that this would make the younger son better. When the grandfather died, they carried the grandmother off and abandoned her, saying that ghosts and wives are not able to live together. The leaders of this state have made this into law and do not treat it as custom, and they have never stopped; to do things like this without choosing, could this really be the way of humaneness and propriety! This is what I call making the behavior convenient and making the customs proper. In the south of Chu there is the state of the people of Yan. When their relatives die they rot their flesh and throw them away, and then afterwards bury the bones, becoming filial sons in this way. In the west of Qin there is the state of Yiqu. When their relatives die, they gather firewood and burn them. As the smoke rises, they call it "ascending into the distance," and in this way they become filial sons. The leaders of these states have made these into law and do not treat them as customs, and they have never stopped; to do things like this without choosing, could this really be the way of humaneness and propriety! This is what I call making the behavior convenient and making the customs proper. If you look at it from these three states, they are all especially miserly. If you look at it from the

gentlemen of the central states, then it would be especially
generous. Like that it would be very generous; like this it
would be very miserly. Still the burials have moderation.
Therefore, food and clothing are what people benefit from
in life, and still there is moderation. Burial is what people
benefit from in death; how could there not be moderation!

Master Mozi's regulations for burial are: a coffin three
inches thick, enough for the decomposing bones; clothing
in three layers, enough for the decomposing flesh; a tomb
dug deep enough so that it doesn't fill with water below
but not so shallow as to allow vapors to come out above;
and a mound high enough to mark the spot, and that is all.
After coming and going weeping, the family should attend
first to the business of their own food and clothing and only
afterwards with sacrifices in order to extend filial offerings
to the relatives. Thus, this is how Master Mozi's law does
not lose the benefit for either the living or the dead.

MOZI

Confucius said, "The gentleperson is pained by the thought of dying and having a name that is not praiseworthy thereafter."

ANALECTS

How do I know that enjoying life is not a delusion? How do I know that hating death is not like a young man going off and not knowing to return?

ZHUANGZI

The grease burns out of the torch but the fire passes on, and we don't know where it will end.

ZHUANGZI

The Master was gravely ill, and Zi Lu made the disciples act as his ministers. When the illness let up a bit, Confucius said, "For a long time indeed has Zi Lu been acting deceitfully, acting as a minister for me when I have no ministers. Who would I fool? Fool heaven? What's more, rather than dying in the hands of ministers, wouldn't I rather die in the hands of my disciples? In fact, rather than getting a great burial, I would rather die in the streets!"

ANALECTS

The present age's burial mounds are as big as mountains, their trees like a forest, and their pavilions and chambers and guest-ways like those of a city. This may be a way to display your wealth to the world, but it is no way to treat the dead. The dead view ten thousand years as the blink of an eye. Even the longest lived do not live past a hundred, and the median don't make it past sixty. If one considers the limitless from the standpoint of a hundred or sixty years, the situations are necessarily different. Only if you adopt the standpoint of the limitless to treat the dead will you get it.

Master Lai said, "A child goes east, west, north, or south, just obeying the commands of its father and mother. How much more so than one's father and mother are the yin and yang to a person. They have brought me close to death, and if I were not to listen I would be savage indeed. What fault do they have in it! The Great Clod transports me with a form, labors me with life, eases me with old age, and rests me with death. Therefore, thinking well of my life, for the same reason I think well of my death. Now when a great blacksmith forges metal, if the metal were to jump up and say, 'I really have to be a Moye sword,' the blacksmith would surely regard it as inauspicious metal. Now once having taken on the form of a man, if I were to say 'Nothing but a man, nothing but a man,' the Creator would surely regard me as an inauspicious person. Now with heaven and earth as the great furnace, with the Creator as the blacksmith, where could I go that wouldn't be acceptable. I will go to sleep soundly and then suddenly I will wake up."

ZHUANGZI.

When Zhuangzi's wife died, Huizi went to console him. Zhuangzi was just then sitting with his legs sprawled out, drumming on a tub and singing. Huizi said, "You lived with her, she brought up your children and grew old. It would be enough just not to weep at her death, but drumming on a tub and singing, this is really too much!" Zhuangzi said, "It is not like this. When she first died, how could I alone be without grief. But then I examined her beginnings and originally she was without life; not only was she without life, but originally she was without form; not only was she without form, but originally she was without breath. Mixed up amidst the jumble and confusion, there was a change and she had breath, the breath changed and she had form, the form changed and she had life. Now there has been another change and she has died. This is just like spring, summer, fall, winter giving way to each other. She's just sleeping peacefully in a huge chamber and my sobbingly following her and weeping for her would show that I don't understand fate. Therefore I stopped."

ZHUANGZI

When Zhuangzi was about to die, his disciple wanted to give him a lavish burial. Zhuangzi said, "I will take heaven and earth as my outer and inner coffins, the sun and moon as my linked jade discs, the stars and constellations as my pearls and beads, and the ten thousand things as my burial offerings. How could it be that the furnishings for my burial are not complete; what is there to add to these?" The disciple said, "I'm afraid that the crows and kites will eat you, Master!" Zhuangzi said, "Above ground I'll be eaten by crows and kites, below ground I'll be eaten by moles and ants. How prejudiced it would be to steal from these and give to those."

ZHUANGZI

Index

Analects 23, 24
  see also Confucius
Art of War see Sunzi

Black Jacket (Zi Yi) 25
Bo Yu 66
Book of the Lord Shang (Shang Jun Shu) 27, 74, 123

Changes, the 129
Chen Kang 66
childhood 6–7
Chunyu Kun 47
Classic of the Way and the Virtue
  see *Laozi (Dao De Jing)*
Confucianism 24, 25, 27–28
Confucius (Kong Qiu/Kongzi) 9, 11, 12, 23, 27
  Analects 23, 24
  on death 158, 162, 163, 168
  on education 50, 52, 53, 58, 59, 66, 67, 68, 69, 70, 71
  on family 36, 37, 40
  on government 111, 115, 123, 126, 130
  and the rites 14
  on sagehood 132, 136–137, 148, 149, 154, 155
  and *shu* 15
  on warfare 86, 87
Constant Prior 94

Da Xue see Great Learning (Da Xue)
dao, the 7, 9–10, 90–105
Dao De Jing see Laozi (Dao De Jing)
Daoism 9, 22, 26, 27
death 7, 158–173
Doctrine of the Mean (Zhong Yong) 25
  see also Zi Si

education 29, 50–71

families 6–7, 34–47
filial piety 36–37, 40–41, 43, 47, 166
Four Books (of Confucianism) 24, 25, 28
funeral rites 163

Gaozi 17, 18, 134
government 106–131
Great Learning (Da Xue) 15–16, 24, 25
  see also Zengzi
Great Way 93
Guodian manuscripts 22
  "Cheng's Hearing of it" 144
  "Six Virtues" 41
  "The Inner Nature Comes from the Mandate" 55

Han Feizi 31
Han Feizi (Han Fei) 15, 27, 29, 30–31

on education 70
on family 44
on government 110, 119, 121, 122, 123, 124, 125, 126, 127
He Guanzi 116
heaven
  effect of 98
  punishment from 153
  son of 106–107
heavenly emotions 95
heavenly and human 96
Helu, king of Wu 23–24
Ho Chi-minh 24
Huan, Duke 63
Hui, king of Liang 118
Hui Shi 18–21
humaneness (*ren*) 11–12, 16, 17, 72, 100, 102
  and government 102
  and sagehood 132, 134, 136, 148
Huang Lao 27

Jesus Christ 10
Ji Kangzi 115
Jing, duke of Qi 162

Kong Congzi 155
Kong Ji *see* Zi Si

Laozi (Dao De Jing/Tao Te Ching) 9, 10, 22, 28
Laozi (Lao Dan) 9, 22
  on the Dao 90, 92, 93, 96, 97, 99
  on death 158
  on education 56
  on family 34
  on government 111, 116, 131
  on sagehood 143, 144, 147, 154, 155
  on warfare 75, 87
Legalism 27, 31
Li Ji (Record of Ritual) 25, 34, 93
Li Si 29
Lie Nü Zhuan 62
Liezi 119, 164
life stages 6–7
Ling, king of Chu 125
love 72
Lü Buwei 29–30
Lü Shi Chunqiu
  on the Dao 99
  on death 162, 169
  on education 55, 56, 59, 63, 68
  on family 41, 45
  on government 131
  on sagehood 145
  on warfare 87

Mao Zedong 24
Mencius 28
Mencius (Meng Ke) 17, 25, 26, 27, 28, 29
   on education 62, 71
   on family 36, 43, 44, 47
   on government 114, 118
   on sagehood 132, 134, 150, 154
   on warfare 75, 82, 83
Mengsun Yang 119
mourning rites 163
Mozi 25
Mozi (Mo Di) 25–26
   on death 166–167
   on government 106–107, 115, 118
   on love 72
   on warfare 89
Mysterious Sameness 97

Neo Confucianism 9

propriety 106, 113

Qinzi 119

reciprocity (*shu*) 14–15
Record of Ritual (Li Ji) 25, 34, 93
Records of the Grand Historian 69, 162
ren see humaneness
rites 12–14, 111
rituals 130

sagehood 28, 116, 132–155
seasonal prohibitions 109
"The Several Disciples Asked" (Mawangdi
   manuscript) 50
Shang Jun Shu (Book of the Lord Shang) 27
Shang Yang (Gongsun Yang) 26–27
   on government 123
   on warfare 74
Shen Buhai 27
   on government 109, 110, 128, 131
Shen Dao 53, 110, 122
Shenzi 27
shu (reciprocity) 14–15
Sou, prince of Yue 125
Strategies of the Warring States 161
Sunzi (Sun Wu) 23–24
Sunzi (Art of War) 24
   on warfare 74, 75, 76, 77, 78, 84, 85, 86

tao see dao
Tao Te Ching see Laozi
three ministers 107
"three in the morning" 102
True Man of Antiquity 103

warfare 23–24, 25–26, 72–89

Warring States period 21
Way, the 9–10, 96, 103, 152
   of heaven and of man 97
Way of the Great 39
Way of ruling 127–128
Wu, lord of Wei 87

Xiang, king of Liang 82
Xiao, Duke 26–27
Xianyang 30
Xuan, king of Qi 114
Xuan, queen of Qin 161
Xunzi 29
Xunzi (Xun Qing) 29
   on the Dao 90, 95, 97, 98, 99
   on death 163
   on education 52, 55, 57, 58, 60, 66–67, 69, 70
   on family 30
   on government 109, 113, 115, 122, 127, 128, 130
   on sagehood 132, 135, 140, 141, 144, 145, 148,
      150, 152–153, 155
   on warfare 74, 76, 81

Yan Hui 12
Yang Zhu 26, 119
yi 16–17
Yi Jing 58

Zengzi (Zeng Shen) 15, 24, 28, 37
   on family 39, 41, 45
   on sagehood 148
Zhao, lord of Han 126
Zheng, king of Qin 30–31
Zhong Yong see Doctrine of the Mean (Zhong Yong)
Zhuangxiang, King 29–30
Zhuangzi, the 28–29
Zhuangzi (Zhuang Zhou) 28–29
   on the Dao 90, 92, 96, 100, 102–105
   and Daoism 9
   on death 168, 170–173
   debate with Hui Shi 18–21
   on education 56, 58, 63, 65, 68
   on family 46
   on government 112, 114, 115, 125, 126, 127
   on sagehood 135, 139, 145, 153, 154, 158
   on warfare 84
Zi Gong 53, 58, 130, 148, 155
Zi Lu 86, 149
Zi Si (Kong Ji) 25, 28
   on the *dao* 96
   on family 34, 36
   on sagehood 141, 149
Zi Yi (Black Jacket) 25
Zuo Zhuan 80

Further reading

Ames, Roger T., and David L. Hall. (trs.) *Focusing the Familiar: A Translation and Philosophical Interpretation of the* Zhongyong. Honolulu: University of Hawaii Press, 2001.

Creel, Herrlee G. *shen Pu-hai: A Chinese Political Philosopher of the Fourth Century BC*. Chicago and London: University of Chicago Press, 1974.

Duyvendak, J.J.L. (tr.) *The Book of Lord Shang: A Classic of the Chinese School of Law*. Original edition, London: Probsthain's Oriental Series 17, 1928. Reprint edition, Clark, New Jersey: Lawbook Exchange, 2003.

Henricks, Robert G. (tr.) *Lao Tzu's* Tao Te Ching: *A Translation of the Startling New Documents Found at Guodian*. Translations from the Asian Classics. New York: Columbia University Press, 2000.

Ivanhoe, Philip J., and Bryan W. Van Norden. (eds.) *Readings in Classical Chinese Philosophy*. 2nd edition. Indianapolis and Cambridge, Mass.: Hackett, 2005.

Knoblock, John. (tr.) *Xunzi: A Translation and Study of the Complete Works*. 3 volumes. Stanford, Cal.: Stanford University Press, 1988–1994.

Knoblock, John, and Jeffrey Riegel. (trs.) *The Annals of Lü Buwei: A Complete Translation and Study*. Stanford, Cal.: Stanford University Press, 2000.

Lau, D.C. (tr.) *Mencius*. Revised edition. New York: Penguin Classics, 2004.

Liao, W.K. *The Complete Works of Han Fei Tzi: A Classic of Chinese Political Science*. London: Arthur Probsthain, 1959.

Mair, Victor H., *et al.* (eds.) *Hawaii Reader in Traditional Chinese Culture*. Honolulu: University of Hawaii Press, 2005.

Sawyer, Ralph D. (tr.) *The Seven Military Classics of Ancient China*. History and Warfare. Boulder, Colo.: Westview, 1993.

Watson, Burton. (tr.) *The Analects of Confucius*. Translations from the Asian Classics. New York: Columbia University Press, 2007.

Watson, Burton. (tr.) *Basic Writings of Mo Tzu, Hsün Tzu, and Han Fei Tzu*. Translations from the Asian Classics. Records of Civilization: Sources and Studies 74. New York: Columbia University Press, 1963.

Watson, Burton. (tr.) *The Complete Works of Chuang Tzu*. Records of Civilization: Sources and Studies 80. New York and London: Columbia University Press, 1970.

About the author

Edward L. Shaughnessy is Creel Professor in Early Chinese Studies, East Asian Languages and Civilizations at the University of Chicago. He was the general editor of *China* (DBP and Oxford University Press, 2005), and his other books include *Ancient China: Life, Myth and Art* (DBP, 2005).

About the photographer

John Cleare is an internationally renowned photographer specializing in mountains and landscapes. His photographs illustrate *Tales from the Tao, Classic Haiku*, and *Teachings of the Buddha* (all DBP), and an edition of the *Tao Te Ching* (Watkins Publishing).